THE SUPER-EASY UK AIR FRYER COOKBOOK FOR BEGINNERS

Easy, Healthy, Mouthwatering Air Fryer
Recipes with Pictures to Fry, Bake and Roast for Home Cooking

Cara Roslin

Copyright © 2023 By Cara Roslin All rights reserved.

No part of this book may be reproduced, transmitted, or distributed in any form or by any means without permission in writing from the publisher except in the case of brief quotations embodied in critical articles or reviews.

Legal & Disclaimer

The content and information in this book is consistent and truthful, and it has been provided for informational, educational and business purposes only.

The illustrations in the book are from the website shutterstock.com, depositphoto.com and freepik.com and have been authorized.

The content and information contained in this book has been compiled from reliable sources, which are accurate based on the knowledge, belief, expertise and information of the Author. The author cannot be held liable for any omissions and/or errors.

TABLE OF
CONTENT

INTRODUCTION	**01**
CHAPTER 1: BREAKFAST	**03**
CHAPTER 2: BEEF	**11**
CHAPTER 3: FISH AND SEAFOOD	**18**
CHAPTER 4: PORK	**25**
CHAPTER 5: VEGETABLES	**34**
CHAPTER 6: LAMB	**41**
CHAPTER 7: SNACK	**49**
CHAPTER 8: DESSERT	**57**
APPENDIX: RECIPES INDEX	**64**

INTRODUCTION

Greetings, my friends,

I'm Cara Roslin. Allow me to take you on a journey through my culinary evolution, one that's deeply intertwined with my love for fried food, a battle with excess weight, and the transformative power of the Ninja Air Fryer. As a food lover since childhood, I vividly recall sneaking into the tantalizing embrace of KFC and McDonald's, indulging in crispy chicken legs and juicy hamburgers. Little did I know that this innocent delight would eventually lead me to a wake-up call about the importance of balance and health.

Fast-forward to college, and my weight had crept up to a staggering 9.3 kg. Reality hit hard, and I realized it was time to reassess my relationship with food. Doctors' stern advice echoed in my ears: control the intake of high-fat and high-calorie foods, and move my body more. With determination, I embarked on a journey of mindful eating and consistent exercise, gradually shedding those excess weight that had held me captive.

Amidst my transformation, fate intervened in the form of a teasing colleague who would later become my wife. As we worked side by side, my dedication to change didn't go unnoticed, catching her attention. It's funny how life twists and turns; that very teasing turned into admiration, and today, we stand united, partners in both love and the kitchen.

Last year, my wife surprised me with a remarkable gift that brought my journey full circle—the Ninja Air Fryer. Its arrival revolutionized my culinary world. No longer did I have to deny myself the pleasures of crispy textures and savoury flavours; instead, I found a healthier way to enjoy the foods I'd cherished since childhood. A spark was ignited, and together, we began creating delicious meals that not only satisfied our taste buds but nourished our bodies too.

And now, I am excited to share my culinary discoveries with you through this cookbook. Born out of a journey that started with a love for fried food, this collection boasts over 100 meticulously tested recipes. Each recipe has been lovingly crafted using UK measurements and ingredients, making it a perfect fit for home cooks like you and me. Whether you're just setting foot in the kitchen or seeking to elevate your culinary prowess, you'll find a diverse array of dishes that cater to all skill levels. But that's not all. In addition to delectable recipes, this cookbook is adorned with vibrant colour pictures that will entice your senses and inspire your creativity.

So, my fellow food enthusiasts, I invite you to join me on this remarkable adventure. Let us celebrate the joy of cooking, the triumph of balance, and the tantalizing possibilities of the Ninja Air Fryer. Through these pages, you'll unlock a world where deliciousness meets wellness, where indulgence finds harmony with health.

As you dive into this cookbook, I wholeheartedly encourage you to immerse yourself in each recipe, explore the art of air frying, and discover the joy of creating wholesome meals that ignite your taste buds and nurture your body. Your culinary journey awaits.

Get ready to embark on a delicious voyage, one that promises to enrich your kitchen experiences and transform the way you enjoy food. Join me in embracing the Ninja Air Fryer's magic, one recipe at a time.

Happy cooking, and bon appétit!

CHAPTER 1
BREAKFAST

Apple Bread Rolls / 4

Avocado Quesadillas / 4

Nugget and Veggie Taco Wraps / 5

Cauliflower with Avocado / 5

Banana Bread / 6

Apple and Walnut Muffins / 6

Grilled Broccoli Frittata / 7

Gammon and Corn Muffins / 7

Coarse Cornmeal and Gammon Fritters / 8

Courgette and Mushroom Bread / 8

Bacon and Broccoli Bread Pudding / 9

Savoury Vegetable Salsa Wraps / 9

British Pumpkin Egg Bake / 10

Luxury Orange Rolls / 10

Apple Bread Rolls

SERVES: 5

PREP TIME: 15 minutes
COOK TIME: 20 minutes

2 green chillies, seeded and chopped
1 bunch coriander, chopped
8 slices bread, brown sides discarded
5 large apples, boiled and mashed
Salt and ground black pepper, to taste
½ tsp. mustard seeds
1 tbsp. olive oil
2 small onions, chopped
2 sprigs curry leaves
½ tsp. turmeric powder

1. Preheat the air fryer to 205ºC.
2. Put the mashed apples in a bowl and sprinkle on salt and pepper. Set to one side.
3. Fry the mustard seeds in olive oil over a medium-low heat in a frying pan, stirring continuously, until they sputter.
4. Add the onions and cook until they turn translucent. Add the curry leaves and turmeric powder and stir. Cook for a further 2 minutes until fragrant.
5. Remove the pan from the heat and combine with the apples. Mix in the green chillies and coriander.
6. Wet the bread slightly and drain of any excess liquid.
7. Spoon a small amount of the apple mixture into the centre of the bread and enclose the bread around the filling, sealing it entirely. Continue until the rest of the bread and filling is used up. Brush each bread roll with some oil and transfer to the basket of the air fryer.
8. Air fry for 15 minutes, gently shaking the air fryer basket at the halfway point to ensure each roll is cooked evenly.
9. Serve immediately.

Avocado Quesadillas

SERVES: 4

PREP TIME: 10 minutes
COOK TIME: 11 minutes

4 tbsps. salsa
57 g Cheddar cheese, grated
½ small avocado, peeled and thinly sliced
1 tin black beans
4 eggs
2 tbsps. skim milk
Salt and ground black pepper, to taste
Cooking spray
4 flour tortillas

1. Preheat the air fryer to 130ºC.
2. Beat together the eggs, milk, salt, and pepper. Spray a baking pan lightly with cooking spray and add egg mixture.
3. Bake for 8 minutes, stirring every 1 to 2 minutes, until eggs are scrambled to the liking. Remove and set aside.
4. Spray one side of each tortilla with cooking spray. Flip over.
5. Divide eggs, salsa, cheese, and avocado among the tortillas, covering only half of each tortilla.
6. Fold each tortilla in half and press down lightly. Increase the temperature of the air fryer to 200ºC.
7. Put 2 tortillas in air fryer basket and air fry for 3 minutes or until cheese melts and outside feels slightly crispy. Repeat with remaining two tortillas.
8. Cut each cooked tortilla into halves. Serve warm.

Nugget and Veggie Taco Wraps

SERVES: 4

PREP TIME: 5 minutes
COOK TIME: 15 minutes

300g grilled maize kernels
4 large flour tortillas
Mixed greens, for garnish
1 tbsp. water
4 pieces commercial vegan nuggets, chopped
1 small brown onion, diced
1 small red pepper, chopped

1. Preheat the air fryer to 200ºC.
2. Over a medium heat, sauté the nuggets in the water with the onion, maize kernels and pepper in a frying pan, then remove from the heat.
3. Fill the tortillas with the nuggets and vegetables and fold them up. Transfer to the inside of the fryer and air fry for 15 minutes.
4. Once crispy, serve immediately, garnished with the mixed greens.

Cauliflower with Avocado

SERVES: 2

PREP TIME: 15 minutes
COOK TIME: 8 minutes

1 ripe medium avocado
½ tsp. garlic powder
¼ tsp. ground black pepper
1 (340-g) steamer bag cauliflower
1 large egg
45 g desiccated Mozzarella cheese
20 g chickpeas

1. Cook cauliflower according to package instructions. Remove from bag and place into cheesecloth or clean towel to remove excess moisture.
2. Place cauliflower into a large bowl and mix the egg and Mozzarella. Cut a piece of parchment to fit your air fryer basket. Separate the cauliflower mixture into two, and place it on the parchment in two mounds. Press out the cauliflower mounds into a ½-cm-thick rectangle. Place the parchment into the air fryer basket.
3. Adjust the temperature to 205ºC and set the timer for 8 minutes.
4. Flip the cauliflower halfway through the cooking time.
5. When the timer beeps, remove the parchment and allow the cauliflower to cool for 5 minutes.
6. Cut open the avocado and remove the pit. Scoop out the inside, place it in a medium bowl, and mash it with garlic powder and pepper. Spread onto the cauliflower. Serve immediately.

CHAPTER 1: BREAKFAST / 5

Banana Bread

SERVES: 3 LOAVES

PREP TIME: 10 minutes
COOK TIME: 22 minutes

190 g plain flour
1 tsp. baking soda
1 tsp. salt
3 ripe bananas, mashed
200 g icing sugar
1 large egg
4 tbsps. unsalted butter, melted

1. Coat the insides of 3 mini loaf pans with cooking spray.
2. In a large mixing bowl, mix the bananas and sugar. In a separate large mixing bowl, combine the egg, butter, flour, baking soda, and salt and mix well.
3. Add the banana mixture to the egg and flour mixture. Mix well. Divide the batter evenly among the prepared pans.
4. Preheat the air fryer to 155°C. Set the mini loaf pans into the air fryer basket.
5. Bake in the preheated air fryer for 22 minutes. Insert a toothpick into the centre of each loaf; if it comes out clean, they are done.
6. When the loaves are cooked through, remove the pans from the air fryer basket. Turn out the loaves onto a wire rack to cool.
7. Serve warm.

Apple and Walnut Muffins

SERVES: 8 MUFFINS

PREP TIME: 15 minutes
COOK TIME: 10 minutes

70 g icing sugar
125 g flour
¼ tsp. ginger
¼ tsp. nutmeg
¼ tsp. baking soda
¼ tsp. salt
1 tsp. baking powder
1 tsp. cinnamon

1 egg
2 tbsps. pancake syrup, plus 2 tsps.
2 tbsps. melted butter, plus 2 tsps.
190 g unsweetened apple sauce
30 g chopped walnuts
45 g diced apple
½ tsp. vanilla extract

1. Preheat the air fryer to 165°C. In a large bowl, stir together the flour, sugar, baking powder, baking soda, salt, cinnamon, ginger, and nutmeg.
2. In a small bowl, beat egg until frothy. Add syrup, butter, apple sauce, and vanilla and mix well.
3. Pour egg mixture into dry ingredients and stir just until moistened.
4. Gently stir in nuts and diced apple.
5. Divide batter among 8 parchment-paper-lined muffin cups.
6. Put 4 muffin cups in air fryer basket and bake for 10 minutes.
7. Repeat with remaining 4 muffins or until toothpick inserted in centre comes out clean.
8. Serve warm.

Grilled Broccoli Frittata

SERVES: 4

PREP TIME: 15 minutes
COOK TIME: 12 minutes

20 g chopped brown onion
30 g chopped green pepper
6 large eggs
50 g chopped broccoli
60 g double whipping cream

1. In a large bowl, whisk eggs and double whipping cream. Mix in broccoli, onion, and pepper.
2. Pour into a 12-cm round oven-safe baking dish. Place baking dish into the air fryer basket.
3. Adjust the temperature to 180°C and set the timer for 12 minutes.
4. Eggs should be firm and cooked fully when the frittata is done. Serve warm.

Gammon and Corn Muffins

SERVES: 8 MUFFINS

PREP TIME: 10 minutes
COOK TIME: 6 minutes

¼ tsp. salt
1 egg, beaten
120 g yellow cornmeal
30 g flour
1½ tsps. baking powder
2 tbsps. rapeseed oil
120 ml milk
120 g desiccated sharp Cheddar cheese
75 g diced gammon

1. Preheat the air fryer to 200°C. In a medium bowl, stir together the cornmeal, flour, baking powder, and salt.
2. Add the egg, oil, and milk to dry ingredients and mix well.
3. Stir in desiccated cheese and diced gammon. Divide batter among 8 parchment-paper-lined muffin cups.
4. Put 4 filled muffin cups in air fryer basket and bake for 5 minutes.
5. Reduce temperature to 165°C and bake for 1 minute or until a toothpick inserted in centre of the muffin comes out clean.
6. Repeat steps 6 and 7 to bake remaining muffins.
7. Serve warm.

Coarse Cornmeal and Gammon Fritters

SERVES: 6 TO 8

PREP TIME: 15 minutes
COOK TIME: 20 minutes

1 egg, beaten
240 g panko bread crumbs
Cooking spray
960 ml water
260 g quick-cooking coarse cornmeal
¼ tsp. salt
2 tbsps. butter
470 g grated Cheddar cheese, divided
150 g finely diced gammon
1 tbsp. chopped chives
Salt and freshly ground black pepper, to taste

1. Bring the water to a boil in a saucepan. Whisk in the coarse cornmeal and ¼ tsp. of salt, and cook for 7 minutes until the coarse cornmeal are soft. Remove the pan from the heat and stir in the butter and 80 g of the grated Cheddar cheese. Transfer the coarse cornmeal to a bowl and let them cool for 10 to 15 minutes.
2. Stir the gammon, chives and the rest of the cheese into the coarse cornmeal and season with salt and pepper to taste. Add the beaten egg and refrigerate the mixture for 30 minutes.
3. Put the panko bread crumbs in a shallow dish. Measure out 60 ml portions of the coarse cornmeal mixture and shape them into patties. Coat all sides of the patties with the panko bread crumbs, patting them with the hands so the crumbs adhere to the patties. You should have about 16 patties. Spritz both sides of the patties with cooking spray.
4. Preheat the air fryer to 205°C.
5. In batches of 5 or 6, air fry the fritters for 8 minutes. Using a flat spatula, flip the fritters over and air fry for another 4 minutes.
6. Serve hot.

Courgette and Mushroom Bread

SERVES: 4

PREP TIME: 10 minutes
COOK TIME: 10 minutes

2 tbsps. softened butter
4 slices bread
110 g soft goat cheese
1 tbsp. olive oil
1 red pepper, cut into strips
2 spring onions, sliced
88 g sliced chestnut mushrooms
1 small courgette, sliced

1. Brush the air fryer basket with the olive oil and preheat the air fryer to 180°C.
2. Put the red pepper, spring onions, mushrooms, and courgette inside the air fryer, give them a stir and air fry for 7 minutes or the vegetables are tender, shaking the basket once throughout the cooking time.
3. Remove the vegetables and set them aside.
4. Spread the butter on the slices of bread and transfer to the air fryer, butter-side up. Brown for 3 minutes.
5. Remove the bread from the air fryer and top with goat cheese and vegetables. Serve warm.

Bacon and Broccoli Bread Pudding

SERVES: 2 TO 4

PREP TIME: 15 minutes
COOK TIME: 48 minutes

240 ml milk
½ tsp. salt
227 g streaky bacon, cut into ½-cm pieces
200 g brioche bread, cut into 1-cm cubes
2 tbsps. butter, melted
3 eggs
Freshly ground black pepper, to taste
70 g frozen broccoli florets, thawed and chopped
125 g grated Swiss cheese

1. Preheat the air fryer to 200°C. Air fry the bacon for 8 minutes until crispy, shaking the basket a few times to help it air fry evenly. Remove the bacon and set it aside on a paper towel.
2. Air fry the brioche bread cubes for 2 minutes to dry and toast lightly.
3. Butter a cake pan. Combine all the ingredients in a large bowl and toss well. Transfer the mixture to the buttered cake pan, cover with aluminium foil and refrigerate the bread pudding overnight, or for at least 8 hours.
4. Remove the cake pan from the refrigerator an hour before you plan to bake and let it sit on the countertop to come to room temperature.
5. Preheat the air fryer to 166°C. Transfer the covered cake pan to the basket of the air fryer, lowering the pan into the basket. Fold the ends of the aluminium foil over the top of the pan before returning the basket to the air fryer.
6. Air fry for 20 minutes. Remove the foil and air fry for an additional 20 minutes. If the top browns a little too much before the custard has set, simply return the foil to the pan. The bread pudding has cooked through when a skewer inserted into the centre comes out clean.
7. Serve warm.

Savoury Vegetable Salsa Wraps

SERVES: 4

PREP TIME: 5 minutes
COOK TIME: 7 minutes

1 head lettuce
130 g salsa
227 g Mozzarella cheese
50 g brown onion, sliced
1 courgette, chopped
1 poblano pepper, deseeded and finely chopped

1. Preheat the air fryer to 200°C. Place the brown onion, courgette, and poblano pepper in the air fryer basket and air fry for 7 minutes, or until they are tender and fragrant.
2. Divide the veggie mixture among the lettuce leaves and spoon the salsa over the top. Finish off with Mozzarella cheese. Wrap the lettuce leaves around the filling.
3. Serve immediately.

British Pumpkin Egg Bake

SERVES: 2

PREP TIME: 10 minutes
COOK TIME: 10 minutes

- 2 eggs
- 120 ml milk
- 1 tsp. cinnamon powder
- 1 tsp. baking soda
- 1 tbsp. olive oil
- 250 g flour
- 2 tbsps. cider vinegar
- 2 tsps. baking powder
- 1 tbsp. icing sugar
- 230 g pumpkin purée

1. Preheat the air fryer to 150°C. Crack the eggs into a bowl and beat with a whisk. Combine with the milk, flour, cider vinegar, baking powder, sugar, pumpkin purée, cinnamon powder, and baking soda, mixing well.
2. Grease a baking tray with oil. Add the mixture and transfer into the air fryer. Bake for 10 minutes.
3. Serve warm.

Luxury Orange Rolls

SERVES: 8

PREP TIME: 15 minutes
COOK TIME: 8 minutes

- 85 g low-fat cream cheese
- 40 g chopped walnuts
- 30 g dried cranberries
- 20 g desiccated, sweetened coconut
- 1 tin organic crescent roll dough
- 1 tbsp. low-fat sour cream or plain yoghurt
- 2 tsps. icing sugar
- ¼ tsp. pure vanilla extract
- ¼ tsp. orange extract
- Butter-flavoured cooking spray

Orange Glaze:
- ¼ tsp. orange extract
- Dash of salt
- 65 g icing sugar
- 1 tbsp. orange juice

1. Cut a circular piece of parchment paper slightly smaller than the bottom of the air fryer basket. Set aside.
2. In a small bowl, combine the cream cheese, sour cream or yoghurt, sugar, and vanilla and orange extracts. Stir until smooth.
3. Preheat the air fryer to 150°C.
4. Separate crescent roll dough into 8 triangles and divide cream cheese mixture among them. Starting at wide end, spread cheese mixture to within 2-cm of point.
5. Sprinkle nuts and cranberries evenly over cheese mixture.
6. Starting at wide end, roll up triangles, then sprinkle with coconut, pressing in lightly to make it stick. Spray tops of rolls with butter-flavoured cooking spray.
7. Put parchment paper in air fryer basket, and place 4 rolls on top, spaced evenly.
8. Air fry for 8 minutes, until rolls are golden brown and cooked through.
9. Repeat steps 7 and 8 to air fry remaining 4 rolls. You should be able to use the same piece of parchment paper twice.
10. In a small bowl, stir together ingredients for glaze and drizzle over warm rolls. Serve warm.

CHAPTER 2
BEEF

Simple New York Strip Steak / 12

Buttered Filet Mignon / 12

Delicious Simple Steaks / 13

Herbed Beef Roast / 13

Simple Beef Burgers / 14

Buttered Rib Eye Steak / 14

Grilled Beef Short Ribs / 15

Beef Roast / 15

Traditional Skirt Steak Strips with Veggies / 16

Gourmet Meatloaf / 16

Steak with Peppers / 16

Crispy Strip Steak / 17

Streaky Rasher Wrapped Filet Mignon / 17

Beef Tips and Onion / 17

Simple New York Strip Steak

SERVES: 2

PREP TIME: 10 minutes
COOK TIME: 10 minutes

Crushed red pepper flakes, to taste
Salt and black pepper, to taste
1 (270 g) New York strip steak
1 tsp. olive oil

1. Preheat the Air fryer to 200°C and grease an Air fryer basket.
2. Rub the steak generously with red pepper flakes, salt and black pepper and coat with olive oil.
3. Transfer the steak in the Air fryer basket and roast for about 10 minutes, flipping once in between.
4. Dish out the steak and cut into desired size slices to serve.

Buttered Filet Mignon

SERVES: 4

PREP TIME: 10 minutes
COOK TIME: 14 minutes

Salt and black pepper, to taste
2 (170 g) filet mignon steaks
15 g butter, softened

1. Preheat the Air fryer to 200°C and grease an Air fryer basket.
2. Rub the steak generously with salt and black pepper and coat with butter.
3. Arrange the steaks in the Air fryer basket and roast for about 14 minutes.
4. Dish out the steaks and cut into desired size slices to serve.

Delicious Simple Steaks

SERVES: 2

PREP TIME: 5 minutes
COOK TIME: 14 minutes

Salt and black pepper, to taste
230 g quality cuts steak

1. Preheat the Air fryer to 200°C and grease an Air fryer basket.
2. Season the steaks evenly with salt and black pepper and transfer into the Air fryer basket.
3. Bake for about 14 minutes and dish out to serve.

Herbed Beef Roast

SERVES: 5

PREP TIME: 10 minutes
COOK TIME: 45 minutes

1 tsp. dried thyme, crushed
Salt, to taste
900 g beef roast
15 ml olive oil
1 tsp. dried rosemary, crushed

1. Preheat the Air fryer to 180°C and grease an Air fryer basket.
2. Rub the roast generously with herb mixture and coat with olive oil.
3. Arrange the roast in the Air fryer basket and roast for about 45 minutes.
4. Dish out the roast and cover with foil for about 10 minutes.
5. Cut into desired size slices and serve.

Simple Beef Burgers

SERVES: 6

PREP TIME: 20 minutes
COOK TIME: 12 minutes

90 ml tomato ketchup
Salt and black pepper, to taste
900 g minced beef
12 Cheddar cheese slices
12 bread rolls

1. Preheat the Air fryer to 200°C and grease an Air fryer basket.
2. Mix the beef, salt and black pepper in a bowl.
3. Make small equal-sized patties from the beef mixture and arrange half of patties in the Air fryer basket.
4. Bake for about 12 minutes and top each patty with 1 cheese slice.
5. Arrange the patties between rolls and drizzle with ketchup.
6. Repeat with the remaining batch and dish out to serve hot.

Buttered Rib Eye Steak

SERVES: 2

PREP TIME: 20 minutes
COOK TIME: 14 minutes

1 tsp. Worcestershire sauce
15 ml olive oil
Salt and black pepper, to taste
115 g unsalted butter, softened
2 tbsps. fresh parsley, chopped
2 (225 g) rib eye steaks
2 tsps. garlic, minced

1. Preheat the Air fryer to 200°C and grease an Air fryer basket.
2. Mix the butter, parsley, garlic, Worcestershire sauce, and salt in a bowl.
3. Place the butter mixture onto a greaseproof paper, roll into a log and refrigerate for about 3 hours.
4. Rub the steak generously with olive oil, salt and black pepper.
5. Arrange the steaks in the Air fryer basket and roast for about 14 minutes, flipping once in between. Dish out the steak onto serving plates and cut into desired size slices.
6. Cut the butter log into slices and top over the steak to serve.

Grilled Beef Short Ribs

SERVES: 8

PREP TIME: 15 minutes
COOK TIME: 16 minutes

1¾ kg bone-in beef short ribs
35 g spring onions, chopped
1 tbsp. fresh ginger, finely grated
15 ml Sriracha
2 tbsps. brown sugar
1 tsp. ground black pepper
235 ml low-sodium soy sauce
115 ml rice vinegar

1. Preheat the Air fryer to 195°C and grease an Air fryer basket.
2. Put the ribs with all other ingredients in a resealable bag and seal the bag. Shake to coat well and refrigerate overnight.
3. Remove the short ribs from resealable bag and arrange in the Air fryer basket in 2 batches.
4. Bake for 8 minutes, flipping once in between and dish out onto a serving platter.
5. Repeat with the remaining ribs and serve hot.

Beef Roast

SERVES: 6

PREP TIME: 10 minutes
COOK TIME: 50 minutes

½ tsp. onion powder
½ tsp. garlic powder
½ tsp. cayenne pepper
½ tsp. ground black pepper
1 kg beef eye of round roast, trimmed
60 ml olive oil
Salt, to taste

1. Preheat the Air fryer to 180°C and grease an Air fryer basket.
2. Rub the roast generously with all the spices and coat with olive oil.
3. Arrange the roast in the Air fryer basket and roast for about 50 minutes.
4. Dish out the roast and cover with foil. Cut into desired size slices and serve.

Traditional Skirt Steak Strips with Veggies

SERVES: 4

PREP TIME: 10 minutes
COOK TIME: 17 minutes

1 (340 g) skirt steak, cut into thin strips
30 ml sauce
40 g honey
Salt and black pepper, to taste
230 g fresh mushrooms, quartered
170 g mangetout
1 onion, cut into half rings
60 ml olive oil, divided

1. Preheat the Air fryer to 200°C and grease an Air fryer basket.
2. Mix 30 ml of oil, soy sauce and honey in a bowl and coat steak strips with this marinade.
3. Put vegetables, remaining oil, salt and black pepper in another bowl and toss well.
4. Transfer the steak strips and vegetables in the Air fryer basket and roast for about 17 minutes.
5. Dish out and serve warm.

Gourmet Meatloaf

SERVES: 4

PREP TIME: 15 minutes
COOK TIME: 25 minutes

400 g lean minced beef
1 chorizo sausage, chopped finely
1 garlic clove, minced
Salt and black pepper, to taste
60 ml olive oil
1 small onion, chopped
25 g fresh breadcrumbs
15 g fresh mushrooms, sliced thinly

1. Preheat the Air fryer to 200°C and grease an Air fryer basket.
2. Mix all the ingredients in a large bowl except mushrooms. Place the beef mixture in the pan and smooth the surface with the back of spatula.
3. Top with mushroom slices and press into the meatloaf gently.
4. Drizzle evenly with oil and arrange in the Air fryer basket.
5. Roast for about 25 minutes and cut into desires size wedges to serve.

Steak with Peppers

SERVES: 4

PREP TIME: 20 minutes
COOK TIME: 22 minutes

560 g beef steak, cut into thin strips
2 green peppers, seeded and cubed
1 tsp. dried oregano, crushed
1 tsp. onion powder
1 tsp. garlic powder
1 tsp. red chilli powder
1 tsp. paprika
Salt, to taste
60 ml olive oil
1 red pepper, seeded and cubed
1 red onion, sliced

1. Preheat the Air fryer to 200°C and grease an Air fryer basket.
2. Mix the oregano and spices in a bowl. Add peppers, onion, oil, and beef strips and mix until well combined.
3. Transfer half of the steak strips in the Air fryer basket and roast for about 11 minutes, flipping once in between.
4. Repeat with the remaining mixture and dish out to serve hot.

Crispy Strip Steak

SERVES: 2

PREP TIME: 15 minutes
COOK TIME: 10 minutes

135 g plain flour
1 tsp. garlic powder
1 tsp. onion powder
Salt and black pepper, to taste
2 eggs
120 g panko bread crumbs
2 (170 g) strip steaks, pounded

1. Preheat the Air fryer to 180°C and grease an Air fryer basket. Place the flour in a shallow bowl and whisk eggs in a second dish.
2. Mix the panko bread crumbs and spices in a third bowl.
3. Rub the steak with flour, dip into the eggs and coat with bread crumb mixture.
4. Transfer the steak in the Air fryer basket and roast for about 10 minutes, flipping once in between.
5. Dish out the steak and cut into desired size slices to serve.

Streaky Rasher Wrapped Filet Mignon

SERVES: 2

PREP TIME: 15 minutes
COOK TIME: 15 minutes

Salt and black pepper, to taste
1 tsp. avocado oil
2 streaky rashers
2 (170 g) filet mignon steaks

1. Preheat the Air fryer to 190°C and grease an Air fryer basket.
2. Wrap each mignon steak with 1 streaky rasher and secure with a toothpick. Season the steak generously with salt and black pepper and coat with avocado oil.
3. Arrange the steaks in the Air fryer basket and roast for about 15 minutes, flipping once in between.
4. Dish out the steaks and cut into desired size slices to serve.

Beef Tips and Onion

SERVES: 2

PREP TIME: 15 minutes
COOK TIME: 10 minutes

450 g beef silverside, cut into 4-cm cubes
½ brown onion, chopped
1 tsp. onion powder
1 tsp. garlic powder
Salt and black pepper, to taste
30 ml Worcestershire sauce
15 ml avocado oil

1. Preheat the Air fryer to 180°C and grease an Air fryer basket.
2. Mix the beef tips, onion, Worcestershire sauce, avocado oil, and spices in a bowl. Arrange the beef mixture in the Air fryer basket and roast for about 10 minutes.
3. Dish out the steak mixture onto serving plates and cut into desired size slices to serve.

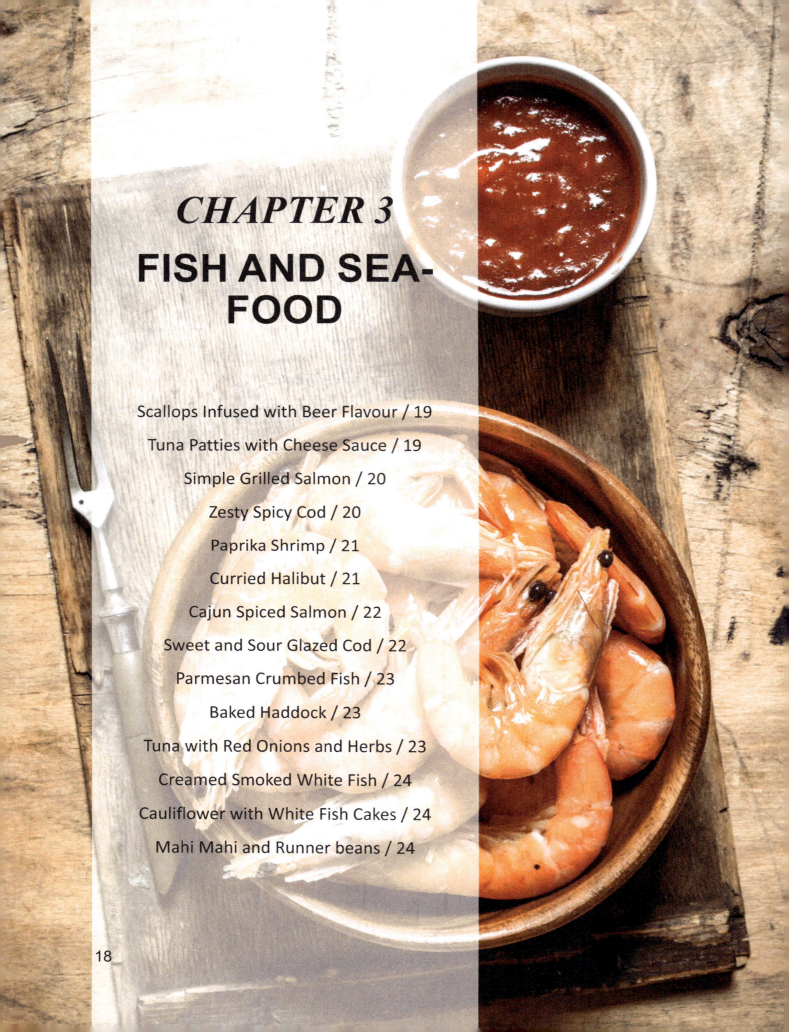

CHAPTER 3
FISH AND SEA-FOOD

Scallops Infused with Beer Flavour / 19

Tuna Patties with Cheese Sauce / 19

Simple Grilled Salmon / 20

Zesty Spicy Cod / 20

Paprika Shrimp / 21

Curried Halibut / 21

Cajun Spiced Salmon / 22

Sweet and Sour Glazed Cod / 22

Parmesan Crumbed Fish / 23

Baked Haddock / 23

Tuna with Red Onions and Herbs / 23

Creamed Smoked White Fish / 24

Cauliflower with White Fish Cakes / 24

Mahi Mahi and Runner beans / 24

Scallops Infused with Beer Flavour

SERVES: 4

PREP TIME: 5 minutes
COOK TIME: 7 minutes

2 sprigs rosemary, only leaves
Sea salt and freshly cracked black pepper, to taste
910 g sea scallops
120 ml beer
4 tbsps. butter

1. In a ceramic dish, mix the sea scallops with beer, let it marinate for 1 hour.
2. Meanwhile, preheat your Air Fryer to 205ºC. Melt the butter and add the rosemary leaves. Stir for a few minutes.
3. Discard the marinade and transfer the sea scallops to the Air Fryer basket. Season with salt and black pepper.
4. Air fry the scallops for 7 minutes, shaking the basket halfway through the cooking time. Work in batches.
5. Serve warm!

Tuna Patties with Cheese Sauce

SERVES: 4

PREP TIME: 15 minutes
COOK TIME: 20 minutes

1 garlic clove, minced
2 tbsps. shallots, minced
100 g Parmesan cheese, grated
455 g tinned tuna, drained
1 egg, whisked
Sea salt and ground black pepper, to taste
1 tbsp. sesame oil
For the Cheese Sauce:
1 tbsp. butter
240 ml beer
2 tbsps. Colby cheese, grated

1. In a mixing bowl, thoroughly combine the tuna, egg, garlic, shallots, Parmesan cheese, salt, and black pepper. Shape the tuna mixture into four patties and place in your refrigerator for 2 hours.
2. Brush the patties with sesame oil on both sides. Roast in the preheated Air Fryer at 180ºC for 14 minutes.
3. In the meantime, melt the butter in a pan over a moderate heat. Add the beer and whisk until it starts bubbling.
4. Now, stir in the grated cheese and bake 3 to 4 minutes longer or until the cheese has melted. Spoon the sauce over the fish cake burgers and serve immediately.

Simple Grilled Salmon

SERVES: 2

PREP TIME: 5 minutes
COOK TIME: 10 minutes

15 ml olive oil
2 (170 g) salmon fillets
Salt and black pepper, as required

1. Preheat the Air fryer to 200°C and grease an Air fryer basket.
2. Season each salmon fillet with salt and black pepper and drizzle with olive oil. Arrange salmon fillets into the Air fryer basket and bake for about 10 minutes.
3. Remove from the Air fryer and dish out the salmon fillets onto the serving plates.

Zesty Spicy Cod

SERVES: 2

PREP TIME: 10 minutes
COOK TIME: 11 minutes

1 tsp. smoked paprika
1 tsp. cayenne pepper
1 tsp. onion powder
1 tsp. garlic powder
2 (170 g) (4-cm thick) cod fillets
Salt and ground black pepper, as required
2 tsps. olive oil

1. Preheat the Air fryer to 200°C and grease an Air fryer basket.
2. Drizzle the cod fillets with olive oil and rub with the all the spices.
3. Arrange the cod fillets into the Air fryer basket and bake for about 11 minutes. Dish out the cod fillets in the serving plates and serve hot.

Paprika Shrimp

SERVES: 2

PREP TIME: 10 minutes
COOK TIME: 10 minutes

½ tsp. smoked paprika
Salt, to taste
450 g tiger shrimps
60 ml olive oil
1 lemon

1. Preheat the Air fryer to 200ºC and grease an Air fryer basket.
2. Mix all the ingredients in a large bowl until well combined.
3. Place the shrimps in the Air fryer basket and air fry for about 10 minutes.
4. Dish out and serve with lemon.

Curried Halibut

SERVES: 4

PREP TIME: 10 minutes
COOK TIME: 10 minutes

2 medium-sized halibut fillets
1 tsp. curry powder
½ tsp. ground coriander
2 eggs
½ tsp. hot paprika
A few drizzles of tabasco sauce
salt and freshly cracked mixed peppercorns, to taste
1½ tbsps. olive oil
20 g asparagus
50 g Parmesan cheese, grated

1. Set your Air Fryer to cook at 185ºC.
2. Then, grab two mixing bowls. In the first bowl, combine the Parmesan cheese with olive oil.
3. In another shallow bowl, thoroughly whisk the egg. Next step, evenly drizzle the halibut fillets with Tabasco sauce, add hot paprika, curry, coriander, salt, and cracked mixed peppercorns.
4. Dip each fish fillet into the whisked egg, now, roll it over the Parmesan mix.
5. Place in a single layer in the Air Fryer cooking basket. Bake for 10 minutes, working in batches. Serve with asparagus if desired.

Cajun Spiced Salmon

SERVES: 2

PREP TIME: 10 minutes
COOK TIME: 8 minutes

½ tsp. caster sugar
15 ml fresh lemon juice
2 (200 g) (2-cm thick) salmon fillets
1 tbsp. Cajun seasoning

1. Preheat the Air fryer to 185ºC and grease an Air fryer grill pan.
2. Season the salmon evenly with Cajun seasoning and sugar.
3. Arrange the salmon fillets into the Air fryer grill pan, skin-side up.
4. Bake for about 8 minutes and dish out the salmon fillets in the serving plates.
5. Drizzle with the lemon juice and serve hot.

Sweet and Sour Glazed Cod

SERVES: 2

PREP TIME: 20 minutes
COOK TIME: 12 minutes

80 ml soy sauce
80 ml honey
3 tsps. rice wine vinegar
1 tsp. water
4 (100 g) cod fillets

1. Preheat the Air fryer to 180ºC and grease an Air fryer basket.
2. Mix the soy sauce, honey, vinegar and water in a small bowl. Reserve about half of the mixture in another bowl.
3. Stir the cod fillets in the remaining mixture until well coated. Cover and refrigerate to marinate for about 3 hours.
4. Arrange the cod fillets into the Air fryer basket and bake for about 12 minutes, flipping once in between.
5. Coat with the reserved marinade and dish out the cod to serve hot.

Parmesan Crumbed Fish

SERVES: 4

PREP TIME: 15 minutes
COOK TIME: 17 minutes

1 tsp. seasoned salt
⅓ tsp. mixed peppercorns
½ tsp. fennel seed
2 eggs, beaten
½ tsp. tarragon
4 fish fillets, halved
2 tbsps. dry white wine
30 g Parmesan cheese, grated

1. Add the Parmesan cheese, salt, peppercorns, fennel seeds, and tarragon to your food processor, blitz for about 20 seconds.
2. Drizzle fish fillets with dry white wine. Dump the egg into a shallow dish.
3. Now, coat the fish fillets with the beaten egg on all sides, then, coat them with the seasoned cracker mix.
4. Air-fry at 175°C for about 17 minutes. Serve warm!

Baked Haddock

SERVES: 2

PREP TIME: 15 minutes
COOK TIME: 13 minutes

2 haddock fillets
¼ tsp. ground black pepper
¼ tsp. cayenne pepper
2 tbsps. olive oil
50 g Parmesan cheese, freshly grated
1 tsp. dried parsley flakes
1 egg, beaten
½ tsp. coarse sea salt

1. Start by preheating your Air Fryer to 180°C. Pat dry the haddock fillets and set aside.
2. In a shallow bowl, thoroughly combine the Parmesan and parsley flakes. Mix until everything is well incorporated.
3. In a separate shallow bowl, whisk the egg with salt, black pepper, and cayenne pepper.
4. Dip the haddock fillets into the egg. Then, dip the fillets into the Parmesan mixture until well coated on all sides.
5. Drizzle the olive oil all over the fish fillets. Lower the coated fillets into the lightly greased Air Fryer basket. Bake for 11 to 13 minutes. Serve warm!

Tuna with Red Onions and Herbs

SERVES: 4

PREP TIME: 10 minutes
COOK TIME: 10 minutes

1 tsp. dried marjoram
1 tbsp. cayenne pepper
½ tsp. sea salt
4 tuna steaks
230 g red onions
4 tsps. olive oil
1 tsp. dried rosemary
½ tsp. black pepper, preferably freshly cracked
1 lemon, sliced

1. Place the tuna steaks in the lightly greased cooking basket. Top with the pearl onions, add the olive oil, rosemary, marjoram, cayenne pepper, salt, and black pepper.
2. Bake in the preheated Air Fryer at 205°C for 9 to 10 minutes. Work in two batches.
3. Serve warm with lemon slices and enjoy!

Creamed Smoked White Fish

SERVES: 4

PREP TIME: 15 minutes
COOK TIME: 13 minutes

½ tbsp. yoghurt
45 g spring garlic, finely chopped
1 tsp. dried rosemary
25 g spring onions, chopped
75 g smoked white fish, chopped
Fresh chopped chives, for garnish
3 eggs, beaten
½ tsp. dried dill
1½ tbsps. fresh cream
1 tsp. salt
1 tsp. dried marjoram
⅓ tsp. ground black pepper, or more to taste
Cooking spray

1. Firstly, spritz four oven safe ramekins with cooking spray. Then, divide smoked whitefish, spring garlic, and spring onions among greased ramekins.
2. Crack an egg into each ramekin, add the cream, yoghurt and all seasonings.
3. Now, air-fry approximately 13 minutes at 180ºC. Taste for doneness and eat warm garnished with fresh chives. Serve warm!

Cauliflower with White Fish Cakes

SERVES: 4

PREP TIME: 10 minutes
COOK TIME: 13 minutes

2 tbsps. butter, room temperature
½ tbsp. coriander, minced
2 tbsps. sour cream
350 g cooked white fish
230 g cauliflower florets
½ tsp. English mustard
Salt and freshly cracked black pepper, to savor

1. Boil the cauliflower until tender. Then, purée the cauliflower in your blender. Transfer to a mixing dish.
2. Now, stir in the fish, coriander, salt, and black pepper.
3. Add the sour cream, English mustard, and butter, mix until everything's well incorporated. Using your hands, shape into patties.
4. Place in the refrigerator for about 2 hours. Roast for 13 minutes at 200ºC. Serve with some extra English mustard.

Mahi Mahi and Runner beans

SERVES: 4

PREP TIME: 15 minutes
COOK TIME: 12 minutes

Salt, as required
2 garlic cloves, minced
30 ml fresh lemon juice
15 ml olive oil
1¼ kilos runner beans
2 tbsps. fresh dill, chopped
4 (170 g) Mahi Mahi fillets
15 ml avocado oil

1. Preheat the Air fryer to 190ºC and grease an Air fryer basket.
2. Mix the runner beans, avocado oil and salt in a large bowl. Arrange runner beans into the Air fryer basket and bake for about 6 minutes.
3. Combine garlic, dill, lemon juice, salt and olive oil in a bowl.
4. Coat Mahi Mahi in this garlic mixture and place on the top of runner beans.
5. Bake for 6 more minutes and dish out to serve warm.

CHAPTER 4
PORK

BBQ Pork Ribs / 26

Vietnamese Pork Chops / 26

Orange Pork Tenderloin / 27

Savoury Mexican Pork Chops / 27

BBQ Pork Steaks / 28

Barbecue Pork Ribs / 28

Simple Pulled Pork / 29

Marinated Pork Tenderloin / 29

Cheddar Bacon Burst and Spinach / 30

Healthy Pork Chop Stir Fry / 30

Roast Citrus Pork Loin / 31

Pork and Aloha Salsa / 31

Cheese Crusted Chops / 32

Pork with Pinto Bean Gorditas / 32

Pork Tenderloin with Radicchio and Endive Salad / 33

BBQ Pork Ribs

SERVES: 4

PREP TIME: 20 minutes
COOK TIME: 35 minutes

½ tsp. mustard powder
½ tsp. freshly ground black pepper
1 tbsp. salt
1 tbsp. dark brown sugar
1 tbsp. sweet paprika
1 tsp. garlic powder
1 tsp. onion powder
1 tsp. poultry seasoning
1 kg individually cut St. Louis–style pork spareribs

1. Preheat the air fryer to 180°C.
2. In a large bowl, whisk together the salt, brown sugar, paprika, garlic powder, onion powder, poultry seasoning, mustard powder, and pepper. Add the ribs and toss. Rub the seasonings into them with your hands until they're fully coated. Set aside for 15 minutes.
3. Arrange the ribs in the air fryer basket, standing up on their ends and leaned up against the wall of the basket and each other. Roast for 35 minutes, or until the ribs are tender inside and golden brown and crisp on the outside. Transfer the ribs to plates and serve hot.

Vietnamese Pork Chops

SERVES: 2

PREP TIME: 15 minutes
COOK TIME: 12 minutes

1 tsp. soy sauce
1 tbsp. brown sugar
1 tbsp. olive oil
1 tsp. ground black pepper
2 pork chops
1 tbsp. chopped shallot
1 tbsp. chopped garlic
1 tbsp. fish sauce
3 tbsps. lemongrass

1. Combine shallot, garlic, fish sauce, lemongrass, soy sauce, brown sugar, olive oil, and pepper in a bowl. Stir to mix well.
2. Put the pork chops in the bowl. Toss to coat well. Place the bowl in the refrigerator to marinate for 2 hours.
3. Preheat the air fryer to 200°C.
4. Remove the pork chops from the bowl and discard the marinade. Transfer the chops into the air fryer.
5. Air fry for 12 minutes or until lightly browned. Flip the pork chops halfway through the cooking time.
6. Remove the pork chops from the basket and serve hot.

Orange Pork Tenderloin

SERVES: 3 TO 4

PREP TIME: 15 minutes
COOK TIME: 23 minutes

2 tbsps. brown sugar
2 tsps. cornflour
½ tsp. soy sauce
2 tsps. grated fresh ginger
60 ml white wine
2 tsps. Dijon mustard
120 ml orange juice
Zest of 1 orange
454 g pork tenderloin
200 g potato wedges
Salt and freshly ground black pepper, to taste
Oranges, halved, for garnish
Fresh parsley, for garnish

1. Combine the brown sugar, cornflour, Dijon mustard, orange juice, soy sauce, ginger, white wine and orange zest in a small saucepan and bring the mixture to a boil on the stovetop. Lower the heat and simmer while you air fry the pork tenderloin or until the sauce has thickened.
2. Preheat the air fryer to 190°C. Season all sides of the pork tenderloin with salt and freshly ground black pepper. Transfer the tenderloin to the air fryer basket.
3. Air fry for 20 to 23 minutes, or until the internal temperature reaches 65°C. Flip the tenderloin over halfway through the cooking process and baste with the sauce.
4. Transfer the tenderloin to a cutting board and let it rest for 5 minutes. Slice the pork at a slight angle and serve garnished with orange halves and fresh parsley. Serve with potato wedges.

Savoury Mexican Pork Chops

SERVES: 2

PREP TIME: 5 minutes
COOK TIME: 15 minutes

5 (113-g) boneless pork chops
2 tbsps. unsalted butter, divided
¼ tsp. dried oregano
1½ tsps. taco seasoning mix

1. Preheat the air fryer to 200°C. Combine the dried oregano and taco seasoning in a small bowl and rub the mixture into the pork chops. Brush the chops with 1 tbsp. butter.
2. In the air fryer, air fry the chops for 15 minutes, turning them over halfway through to air fry on the other side.
3. When the chops are a brown colour, check the internal temperature has reached 65°C and remove from the air fryer. Serve with a garnish of remaining butter.

BBQ Pork Steaks

SERVES: 4

PREP TIME: 5 minutes
COOK TIME: 15 minutes

4 pork steaks
1 tbsp. vinegar
1 tsp. soy sauce
110 g brown sugar
120 g ketchup
1 tbsp. Cajun seasoning
2 tbsps. BBQ sauce

1. Preheat the air fryer to 180°C. Sprinkle pork steaks with Cajun seasoning. Combine remaining ingredients and brush onto steaks.
2. Add coated steaks to air fryer. Air fry for 15 minutes until just browned.
3. Serve immediately.

Barbecue Pork Ribs

SERVES: 4

PREP TIME: 5 minutes
COOK TIME: 30 minutes

1 tbsp. barbecue dry rub
1 tsp. sesame oil
454 g pork ribs, chopped
1 tsp. mustard
1 tbsp. apple cider vinegar

1. Combine the dry rub, mustard, apple cider vinegar, and sesame oil, then coat the ribs with this mixture. Refrigerate the ribs for 20 minutes.
2. Preheat the air fryer to 180°C.
3. When the ribs are ready, place them in the air fryer and air fry for 15 minutes. Flip them and air fry on the other side for a further 15 minutes.
4. Serve immediately.

Simple Pulled Pork

SERVES: 1

PREP TIME: 5 minutes
COOK TIME: 24 minutes

454 g pork tenderloin
2 tbsps. barbecue dry rub
80 g lime
1 tsp. butter

1. Preheat the air fryer to 190°C. Massage the dry rub into the tenderloin, coating it well.
2. Air fry the tenderloin in the air fryer for 20 minutes. When air fried, shred with two forks.
3. Add the butter into the air fryer along with the desiccated pork and stir well. Air fry for a further 4 minutes.
4. Allow to cool, then serve with lime wedges.

Marinated Pork Tenderloin

SERVES: 4 TO 6

PREP TIME: 10 minutes
COOK TIME: 30 minutes

60 ml olive oil
60 ml soy sauce
60 ml freshly squeezed lemon juice
1 tsp. salt
½ tsp. freshly ground black pepper
907 g pork tenderloin
1 garlic clove, minced
1 tbsp. Dijon mustard

1. In a large mixing bowl, make the marinade: Mix the olive oil, soy sauce, lemon juice, minced garlic, Dijon mustard, salt, and pepper. Reserve ¼ cup of the marinade.
2. Put the tenderloin in a large bowl and pour the remaining marinade over the meat. Cover and marinate in the refrigerator for about 1 hour.
3. Preheat the air fryer to 200°C.
4. Put the marinated pork tenderloin into the air fryer basket. Roast for 10 minutes. Flip the pork and baste it with half of the reserved marinade. Roast for 10 minutes more.
5. Flip the pork, then baste with the remaining marinade. Roast for another 10 minutes, for a total cooking time of 30 minutes.
6. Serve immediately.

CHAPTER 4: PORK / 29

Cheddar Bacon Burst and Spinach

SERVES: 8

PREP TIME: 5 minutes
COOK TIME: 60 minutes

30 rasher of bacon
208 g Cheddar cheese
120 g raw spinach
1 tbsp. Chipotle seasoning
2 tsps. Italian seasoning

1. Preheat the air fryer to 190°C. Weave the bacon into 15 vertical pieces and 12 horizontal pieces. Cut the extra 3 in half to fill in the rest, horizontally.
2. Season the bacon with Chipotle seasoning and Italian seasoning.
3. Add the cheese to the bacon. Add the spinach and press down to compress. Tightly roll up the woven bacon.
4. Line a baking sheet with kitchen foil and add plenty of salt to it.
5. Put the bacon on top of a cooling rack and put that on top of the baking sheet. Bake for 60 minutes.
6. Let cool for 15 minutes before slicing and serve.

Healthy Pork Chop Stir Fry

SERVES: 4

PREP TIME: 10 minutes
COOK TIME: 20 minutes

1 tbsp. olive oil
¼ tsp. ground black pepper
½ tsp. salt
1 egg white
2 sliced spring onions
2 tbsps. olive oil
¼ tsp. ground white pepper
1 tsp. sea salt
4 (113-g) pork chops
72 g almond flour
2 sliced red chilli

1. Coat the air fryer basket with olive oil. Whisk black pepper, salt, and egg white together until foamy.
2. Cut pork chops into pieces, leaving just a bit on bones. Pat dry.
3. Add pieces of pork to egg white mixture, coating well. Let sit for marinade 20 minutes.
4. Preheat the air fryer to 180°C. Put marinated chops into a large bowl and add almond flour. Dredge and shake off excess and place into air fryer.
5. Air fry the chops in the preheated air fryer for 12 minutes.
6. Turn up the heat to 200°C and air fry for another 6 minutes until pork chops are nice and crisp.
7. Meanwhile, remove red chilli and chop up. Chop spring onions and mix with red chilli pieces.
8. Heat a frying pan with olive oil. Stir-fry the white pepper, salt, spring onions, and red chilli 60 seconds. Then add fried pork pieces to skills and toss with spring onion mixture. Stir-fry 1 to 2 minutes until well coated and hot.
9. Serve immediately.

Roast Citrus Pork Loin

SERVES: 8

PREP TIME: 10 minutes
COOK TIME: 45 minutes

1 tsp. dried lemongrass
907 g boneless pork loin roast
Salt and ground black pepper, to taste
Cooking spray
1 tbsp. lime juice
1 tbsp. orange marmalade
1 tsp. coarse brown mustard
1 tsp. curry powder

1. Preheat the air fryer to 180°C. Mix the lime juice, marmalade, mustard, curry powder, and lemongrass.
2. Rub mixture all over the surface of the pork loin. Season with salt and pepper.
3. Spray air fryer basket with cooking spray and place pork roast diagonally in the basket.
4. Air fry for approximately 45 minutes, until the internal temperature reaches at least 65°C.
5. Wrap roast in foil and let rest for 10 minutes before slicing.
6. Serve immediately.

Pork and Aloha Salsa

SERVES: 4

PREP TIME: 20 minutes
COOK TIME: 8 minutes

2 eggs
2 tbsps. milk
454 g boneless, thin pork cutlets (1-cm thick)
Lemon pepper and salt, to taste
30 g cornflour
30 g flour
30 g panko bread crumbs
4 tsps. sesame seeds
Cooking spray
For the Aloha Salsa:
1 tsp. low-sodium soy sauce
⅛ tsp. crushed red pepper
⅛ tsp. ground black pepper
225 g fresh pineapple, chopped in small pieces
15 g red onion, finely chopped
30 g green or red pepper, chopped
½ tsp. ground cinnamon

1. In a medium bowl, stir together all ingredients for salsa. Cover and refrigerate while cooking the pork.
2. Preheat the air fryer to 200°C. Beat the eggs and milk in a shallow dish.
3. In another shallow dish, mix the flour, panko, and sesame seeds.
4. Sprinkle pork cutlets with lemon pepper and salt.
5. Dip pork cutlets in cornflour, egg mixture, and then panko coating. Spray both sides with cooking spray.
6. Air fry the cutlets for 3 minutes. Turn cutlets over, spraying both sides, and continue air frying for 5 minutes or until well done.
7. Serve fried cutlets with salsa on the side.

Cheese Crusted Chops

SERVES: 4 TO 6

PREP TIME: 10 minutes
COOK TIME: 12 minutes

- 1 tsp. smoked paprika
- 2 beaten eggs
- 3 tbsps. grated Parmesan cheese
- Cooking spray
- ¼ tsp. pepper
- ½ tsp. salt
- ¼ tsp. chilli powder
- ½ tsp. onion powder
- 4 to 6 thick boneless pork chops
- 110 g pork rind crumbs

1. Preheat the air fryer to 200°C. Rub the pepper and salt on both sides of pork chops.
2. In a food processor, pulse pork rinds into crumbs. Mix crumbs with chilli powder, onion powder, and paprika in a bowl.
3. Beat eggs in another bowl. Dip pork chops into eggs then into pork rind crumb mixture.
4. Spritz the air fryer with cooking spray and add pork chops to the basket.
5. Air fry for 12 minutes. Serve garnished with the Parmesan cheese.

Pork with Pinto Bean Gorditas

SERVES: 4

PREP TIME: 20 minutes
COOK TIME: 21 minutes

- 1 tsp. dried oregano
- 2 tsps. paprika
- 1 tsp. garlic powder
- 454 g lean pork mince
- 2 tbsps. chilli powder
- 2 tbsps. ground cumin
- 120 ml water
- 1 (425-g) tin pinto beans, drained and rinsed
- 117 g taco sauce
- Salt and freshly ground black pepper, to taste
- 470 g grated Cheddar cheese
- 5 (24-cm) flour tortillas
- 4 (16-cm) crispy flour tortilla shells
- 60 g desiccated lettuce
- 1 tomato, diced
- 60 g sliced black olives
- Sour cream, for serving
- Tomato salsa, for serving
- Cooking spray

1. Preheat the air fryer to 200°C. Spritz the air fryer basket with cooking spray.
2. Put the pork mince in the air fryer basket and air fry at 200°C for 10 minutes, stirring a few times to gently break up the meat. Combine the chilli powder, cumin, oregano, paprika, garlic powder and water in a small bowl. Stir the spice mixture into the browned pork. Stir in the beans and taco sauce and air fry for an additional minute. Transfer the pork mixture to a bowl. Season with salt and freshly ground black pepper.
3. Sprinkle 40 g of the grated cheese in the centre of the flour tortillas, leaving a 4-cm border around the edge free of cheese and filling. Divide the pork mixture among the four tortillas, placing it on top of the cheese. Put a crunchy flour tortilla on top of the pork and top with desiccated lettuce, diced tomatoes, and black olives. Cut the remaining flour tortilla into 4 quarters. These quarters of tortilla will serve as the bottom of the gordita. Put one quarter tortilla on top of each gordita and fold the edges of the bottom flour tortilla up over the sides, enclosing the filling. While holding the seams down, brush the bottom of the gordita with olive oil and place the seam side down on the countertop while you finish the remaining three gorditas.
4. Preheat the air fryer to 190°C.
5. Air fry one gordita at a time. Transfer the gordita carefully to the air fryer basket, seam side down. Brush or spray the top tortilla with oil and air fry for 5 minutes. Carefully turn the gordita over and air fry for an additional 4 to 5 minutes until both sides are browned. When finished air frying all four gorditas, layer them back into the air fryer for an additional minute to make sure they are all warm before serving with sour cream and salsa.

Pork Tenderloin with Radicchio and Endive Salad

SERVES: 4

PREP TIME: 25 minutes
COOK TIME: 7 minutes

1 (227-g) pork tenderloin
Salt and freshly ground black pepper, to taste
30 g flour
1 tsp. dry mustard
1 tsp. garlic powder
1 tsp. dried thyme
1 tsp. salt
2 eggs, lightly beaten
80 g crushed crackers
1 tsp. paprika
vegetable or rapeseed oil, in spray bottle
For the Vinaigrette:
60 ml white balsamic vinegar
2 tbsps. agave syrup (or honey or maple syrup)
1 tbsp. Dijon mustard
juice of ½ lemon
2 tbsps. chopped chervil or flat-leaf parsley
1 heart romaine lettuce, torn into large pieces
½ head radicchio, coarsely chopped
2 heads endive, sliced
100 g cherry tomatoes, halved
85 g fresh Mozzarella, diced
Salt and freshly ground black pepper, to taste
salt and freshly ground black pepper
120 ml extra-virgin olive oil
Radicchio and Endive Salad:

1. Slice the pork tenderloin into 2-cm slices. Using a meat pounder, pound the pork slices into thin 1-cm medallions. Generously season the pork with salt and freshly ground black pepper on both sides.
2. Set up a dredging station using three shallow dishes. Put the flour in one dish and the beaten eggs in a second dish. Combine the cracker meal, paprika, dry mustard, garlic powder, thyme and salt in a third dish.
3. Preheat the air fryer to 200°C.
4. Dredge the pork medallions in flour first and then into the beaten egg. Let the excess egg drip off and coat both sides of the medallions with the cracker meal crumb mixture. Spray both sides of the coated medallions with vegetable or rapeseed oil.
5. Air fry the medallions in two batches at 200°C for 5 minutes. Once you have air-fried all the medallions, flip them all over and return the first batch of medallions back into the air fryer on top of the second batch. Air fry at 200°C for an additional 2 minutes.
6. While the medallions are cooking, make the salad and dressing. Whisk the white balsamic vinegar, agave syrup, Dijon mustard, lemon juice, chervil, salt and pepper together in a small bowl. Whisk in the olive oil slowly until combined and thickened.
7. Combine the romaine lettuce, radicchio, endive, cherry tomatoes, and Mozzarella cheese in a large salad bowl. Drizzle the dressing over the vegetables and toss to combine. Season with salt and freshly ground black pepper.
8. Serve the pork medallions warm on or beside the salad.

CHAPTER 5
VEGETABLES

Incredibly Crunchy Tofu / 35

Delicious Peppers Cups / 35

Easy Glazed Carrots / 36

Courgette and Mushroom Kebab / 36

Asparagus Bundles Enveloped in Crunchy Bacon Strips / 37

Aubergine with Tomato and Cheese / 37

Delicious Roasted Mushrooms / 38

Spinach Cheese Casserole / 38

Mushrooms with Peas / 39

Veggie-filled Pumpkin Basket / 39

Homemade Favourite Potatoes / 39

Cold Salad with Pasta and Veggies / 40

Fried Fresh Veggie Medley / 40

Roast Aubergine with Courgette Bites / 40

Incredibly Crunchy Tofu

SERVES: 4

PREP TIME: 15 minutes
COOK TIME: 30 minutes

1 chicken stock cube, crushed
2 tbsps. low-sodium soy sauce
2 tbsps. fish sauce
1 tsp. sesame oil
340 g extra-firm tofu, drained and cubed into 2.5-cm size
1 tsp. butter

1. Preheat the Air fryer to 180°C and grease an Air fryer basket.
2. Mix soy sauce, fish sauce, sesame oil and crushed chicken stock cube in a bowl and toss to coat well.
3. Stir in the tofu cubes and mix until well combined.
4. Keep aside to marinate for about 30 minutes and then transfer into Air fryer basket.
5. Air fry for about 30 minutes, flipping every 10 minutes and serve hot.

Delicious Peppers Cups

SERVES: 4

PREP TIME: 10 minutes
COOK TIME: 8 minutes

½ tbsp. olive oil
Freshly ground black pepper, to taste
8 mini red peppers, tops and seeds removed
85 g feta cheese, crumbled
1 tsp. fresh parsley, chopped

1. Preheat the Air fryer to 200°C and grease an Air fryer basket.
2. Mix feta cheese, parsley, olive oil and black pepper in a bowl.
3. Stuff the peppers with feta cheese mixture and arrange in the Air fryer basket.
4. Bake for about 8 minutes and dish out to serve hot.

Easy Glazed Carrots

SERVES: 4

PREP TIME: 10 minutes
COOK TIME: 12 minutes

20 g honey
Salt and black pepper, to taste
225 g carrots, peeled and cut into large chunks
15 ml olive oil

1. Preheat the Air fryer to 200ºC and grease an Air fryer basket.
2. Mix all the ingredients in a bowl and toss to coat well.
3. Transfer into the Air fryer basket and bake for about 12 minutes.
4. Dish out and serve hot.

Courgette and Mushroom Kebab

SERVES: 8 SKEWERS

PREP TIME: 40 minutes
COOK TIME: 8 minutes

70 g basil pesto
½ tsp. salt
¼ tsp. ground black pepper
1 medium courgette, trimmed and cut into 1-cmslices
½ medium brown onion, peeled and cut into 2-cmsquares
1 medium red pepper, seeded and cut into 2-cmsquares
16 whole chestnut mushrooms

1. Divide courgette slices, onion, and pepper into eight even portions. Place on 12-cm skewers for a total of eight kebabs. Add 2 mushrooms to each skewer and brush kebabs generously with pesto.
2. Sprinkle each kebab with salt and black pepper on all sides, then place into ungreased air fryer basket. Adjust the temperature to 190ºC and set the timer for 8 minutes, turning kebabs halfway through cooking. Vegetables will be browned at the edges and tender-crisp when done. Serve warm.

Asparagus Bundles Enveloped in Crunchy Bacon Strips

SERVES: 4

PREP TIME: 20 minutes
COOK TIME: 8 minutes

450 g asparagus
1 tbsps. brown sugar
20 ml olive oil
½ tbsp. sesame oil, toasted
4 streaky rashers of bacon
½ tbsp. sesame seeds, toasted
1 garlic clove, minced

1. Preheat the Air fryer to 180ºC and grease an Air fryer basket.
2. Mix garlic, brown sugar, olive oil and sesame oil in a bowl till sugar is dissolved.
3. Divide asparagus into 4 equal bunches and wrap a streaky rasher slice around each bunch.
4. Rub the asparagus bunch with garlic mixture and arrange in the Air fryer basket.
5. Sprinkle with sesame seeds and roast for about 8 minutes.
6. Dish out and serve hot.

Aubergine with Tomato and Cheese

SERVES: 4

PREP TIME: 35 minutes
COOK TIME: 5 minutes

1 aubergine, peeled and sliced
2 peppers, seeded and sliced
1 tsp. smoked paprika
Salt and ground black pepper, to taste
1 tomato, sliced
1 red onion, sliced
1 tsp. fresh garlic, minced
4 tbsps. olive oil
1 tsp. mustard
1 tsp. dried oregano
170 g halloumi cheese, sliced lengthways

1. Start by preheating your Air Fryer to 190ºC. Spritz a baking pan with nonstick cooking spray.
2. Place the aubergine, peppers, onion, and garlic on the bottom of the baking pan. Add the olive oil, mustard, and spices. Transfer to the cooking basket and bake 14 minutes.
3. Top with the tomatoes and cheese, increase the temperature to 200ºC and bake for 5 minutes or more until bubbling. Let it sit on a cooling rack for 10 minutes before serving.
4. Serve warm!

CHAPTER 5: VEGETABLES / 37

Delicious Roasted Mushrooms

SERVES: 4

PREP TIME: 10 minutes
COOK TIME: 32 minutes

15 g butter
2 tsps. herbs de Provence
½ tsp. garlic powder
900 g mushrooms, quartered
30 ml white vermouth

1. Preheat the Air fryer to 160°C and grease an Air fryer pan.
2. Mix herbs de Provence, garlic powder and butter in the Air fryer pan and transfer into the Air fryer basket.
3. Roast for about 2 minutes and stir in the mushrooms.
4. Roast for about 25 minutes and add white vermouth.
5. Roast for about 5 more minutes and dish out to serve warm.

Spinach Cheese Casserole

SERVES: 4

PREP TIME: 15 minutes
COOK TIME: 15 minutes

25 g chopped pickled red chilli
60 g fresh spinach, chopped
215 g cauliflower florets, chopped
175 g artichoke hearts, chopped
1 tbsp. salted butter, melted
15 g diced brown onion
230 g full-fat cream cheese, softened
65 g full-fat mayonnaise
70 g full-fat sour cream

1. In a large bowl, mix butter, onion, cream cheese, mayonnaise, and sour cream. Fold in red chilli, spinach, cauliflower, and artichokes.
2. Pour the mixture into a round baking dish. Cover with foil and place into the air fryer basket.
3. Adjust the temperature to 190°C and set the timer for 15 minutes.
4. In the last 2 minutes of cooking, remove the foil to brown the top. Serve warm.

Mushrooms with Peas

SERVES: 4

PREP TIME: 15 minutes
COOK TIME: 15 minutes

450 g chestnut mushrooms, halved
4 garlic cloves, finely chopped
2 tsps. Chinese five spice powder
½ tsp. ground ginger
70 g frozen peas
115 ml rice vinegar
115 ml soy sauce
115 ml maple syrup

1. Preheat the Air fryer to 175°C and grease an Air fryer pan.
2. Mix soy sauce, maple syrup, vinegar, garlic, five spice powder, and ground ginger in a bowl.
3. Arrange the mushrooms in the Air fryer basket and roast for about 10 minutes.
4. Stir in the soy sauce mixture and peas and roast for 5 more minutes.
5. Dish out the mushroom mixture in plates and serve hot.

Veggie-filled Pumpkin Basket

SERVES: 6

PREP TIME: 15 minutes
COOK TIME: 30 minutes

1 pumpkin, seeded
2 garlic cloves, minced
2 tsps. herb mix
1 sweet potato, peeled and chopped
1 parsnip, peeled and chopped
70 g peas, shelled
1 onion, chopped

1. Preheat the Air fryer to 180°C and grease an Air fryer basket.
2. Mix all the ingredients in a bowl except pumpkin and toss to coat well.
3. Stuff the vegetable mixture half way into the pumpkin and transfer into the Air fryer basket.
4. Bake for about 30 minutes and dish out to serve warm.

Homemade Favourite Potatoes

SERVES: 4

PREP TIME: 10 minutes
COOK TIME: 20 minutes

340 g waxy potatoes, cubed and boiled
60 ml olive oil, divided
1 tbsp. paprika, divided
Salt and black pepper, to taste
170 g Greek plain yoghurt

1. Preheat the Air fryer to 180°C and grease an Air fryer basket.
2. Mix 15 ml olive oil, ⅓ tbsp. of paprika and black pepper in a bowl and toss with potatoes to coat well.
3. Transfer into the Air fryer basket and roast for about 20 minutes.
4. Mix yoghurt, remaining oil, salt and black pepper in a bowl and serve with potatoes.

Cold Salad with Pasta and Veggies

SERVES: 12

PREP TIME: 30 minutes
COOK TIME: 1 hour 35 minutes

- 3 medium courgettes, sliced into 1-cm thick rounds
- 70 g Parmesan cheese, grated
- 60 ml olive oil, divided
- 115 ml fat-free Italian dressing
- Salt, to taste
- 3 small aubergines, sliced into 1-cm rounds
- 4 medium tomatoes, cut in eighths
- 1½ kg cooked pasta

1. Preheat the Air fryer to 180°C and grease an Air fryer basket.
2. Mix courgette and 15 ml of olive oil in a bowl and toss to coat well.
3. Arrange the courgette slices in the Air fryer basket and bake about 25 minutes.
4. Mix aubergines and 15 ml of olive oil in another bowl and toss to coat well.
5. Arrange the aubergine slices in the Air fryer basket and bake about 40 minutes.
6. Set the Air fryer to 160°C and place tomatoes into the prepared basket.
7. Bake for about 30 minutes and combine all the Air fried vegetables.
8. Stir in the remaining ingredients and refrigerate covered for at least 2 hours to serve.

Fried Fresh Veggie Medley

SERVES: 4

PREP TIME: 10 minutes
COOK TIME: 15 minutes

- 2 yellow peppers, seeded and chopped
- 2 small onions, chopped
- 2 garlic cloves, minced
- 2 tbsps. herbs de Provence
- 15 ml olive oil
- 15 ml balsamic vinegar
- Salt and black pepper, to taste
- 1 aubergine, chopped
- 1 courgette, chopped
- 3 tomatoes, chopped

1. Preheat the Air fryer to 180°C and grease an Air fryer basket.
2. Mix all the ingredients in a bowl and toss to coat well.
3. Transfer into the Air fryer basket and bake about 15 minutes.
4. Keep in the Air fryer for about 5 minutes and dish out to serve hot.

Roast Aubergine with Courgette Bites

SERVES: 8

PREP TIME: 35 minutes
COOK TIME: 30 minutes

- 455 g aubergine, peeled and cubed
- 455 g courgette, peeled and cubed
- 3 tbsps. olive oil
- 2 tsps. fresh mint leaves, chopped
- 1½ tsps. red pepper chilli flakes
- 2 tbsps. melted butter

1. Toss all of the above ingredients in a large-sized mixing dish.
2. Roast the aubergine and Courgette bites for 30 minutes at 160°C in your Air Fryer, turning once or twice.
3. Serve with a homemade dipping sauce.

CHAPTER 6
LAMB

Lime Marinated Lamb Chop / 42

Grilled Lamb Ribs / 42

Lamb leg with Brussels Sprouts / 43

Roasted Lamb / 43

Quick Lamb Satay / 44

Mustard Lamb Loin Chops / 44

Herbed Lamb Chops / 45

Simple Lamb Chops / 45

Za'atar Lamb Loin Chops / 46

Pesto Coated Lamb Rack / 46

Spiced Lamb Steaks / 46

Lollipop Lamb Chops / 47

Savoury Lamb Meatballs / 47

Herbed Lamb Chops and Parmesan / 48

Easy Lamb Burger / 48

Lime Marinated Lamb Chop

SERVES: 2

PREP TIME: 5 minutes
COOK TIME: 5 minutes

4 (2-cm thick) lamb chops
15 g chopped fresh mint leaves
4 cloves garlic, roughly chopped
2 tsps. fine sea salt
½ tsp. ground black pepper
Sprigs of fresh mint, for garnish (optional)
Lime slices, for serving (optional)
Marinade:
2 tsps. grated lime zest
120 ml lime juice
60 ml avocado oil

1. Make the marinade: Place all the ingredients for the marinade in a food processor or blender and purée until mostly smooth with a few small chunks. Transfer half of the marinade to a shallow dish and set the other half aside for serving. Add the lamb to the shallow dish, cover, and place in the refrigerator to marinate for at least 2 hours or overnight.
2. Spray the air fryer basket with avocado oil. Preheat the air fryer to 200°C.
3. Remove the chops from the marinade and place them in the air fryer basket. Bake for 5 minutes, or until the internal temperature reaches 60°C for medium doneness.
4. Allow the chops to rest for 10 minutes before serving with the rest of the marinade as a sauce. Garnish with fresh mint leaves and serve with lime slices, if desired. Best served fresh.

Grilled Lamb Ribs

SERVES: 4

PREP TIME: 5 minutes
COOK TIME: 18 minutes

2 tbsps. mustard
Salt and ground black pepper, to taste
15 g mint leaves, chopped
280 g Greek yoghurt
454 g lamb ribs
1 tsp. rosemary, chopped

1. Preheat the air fryer to 180°C. Use a brush to apply the mustard to the lamb ribs, and season with rosemary, salt, and pepper.
2. Air fry the ribs in the air fryer for 18 minutes.
3. Meanwhile, combine the mint leaves and yoghurt in a bowl.
4. Remove the lamb ribs from the air fryer when cooked and serve with the mint yoghurt.

42 \ CHAPTER 6: LAMB

Lamb leg with Brussels Sprouts

SERVES: 6

PREP TIME: 20 minutes
COOK TIME: 1 hour 30 minutes

1 kg leg of lamb
1 tbsp. fresh rosemary, minced
1 garlic clove, minced
Salt and ground black pepper, as required
40 g honey
1 tbsp. fresh lemon thyme
680 g Brussels sprouts, trimmed
45 ml olive oil, divided

1. Preheat the Air fryer to 150°C and grease an Air fryer basket.
2. Make slits in the leg of lamb with a sharp knife.
3. Mix 30 ml of oil, herbs, garlic, salt, and black pepper in a bowl.
4. Coat the leg of lamb with oil mixture generously and arrange in the Air fryer basket.
5. Roast for about 75 minutes and set the Air fryer to 200°C.
6. Coat the Brussels sprout evenly with the remaining oil and honey and arrange them in the Air fryer basket with leg of lamb.
7. Roast for about 15 minutes and dish out to serve warm.

Roasted Lamb

SERVES: 4

PREP TIME: 15 minutes
COOK TIME: 1 hour 30 minutes

1¼-kg half lamb leg roast, slits carved
15 ml olive oil
Cracked Himalayan rock salt and cracked peppercorns, to taste
2 garlic cloves, sliced into smaller slithers
1 tbsp. dried rosemary

1. Preheat the Air fryer to 200°C and grease an Air fryer basket.
2. Insert the garlic slithers in the slits and brush with rosemary, oil, salt, and black pepper.
3. Arrange the lamb in the Air fryer basket and roast for about 15 minutes.
4. Set the Air fryer to 175°C on the Roast mode and roast for 1 hour and 15 minutes.
5. Dish out the lamb and serve hot.

Quick Lamb Satay

SERVES: 2

PREP TIME: 5 minutes
COOK TIME: 8 minutes

Salt and ground black pepper, to taste
2 boneless lamb steaks
Cooking spray
¼ tsp. cumin
1 tsp. ginger
½ tsp. nutmeg

1. Combine the cumin, ginger, nutmeg, salt and pepper in a bowl.
2. Cube the lamb steaks and massage the spice mixture into each one.
3. Leave to marinate for 10 minutes, then transfer onto metal skewers.
4. Preheat the air fryer to 200ºC. Spritz the skewers with the cooking spray, then air fry them in the air fryer for 8 minutes.
5. Take care when removing them from the air fryer and serve.

Mustard Lamb Loin Chops

SERVES: 4

PREP TIME: 15 minutes
COOK TIME: 30 minutes

8 (115 g) lamb loin chops
½ tsp. olive oil
1 tsp. dried tarragon
Salt and black pepper, to taste
2 tbsps. Dijon mustard
15 ml fresh lemon juice

1. Preheat the Air fryer to 200ºC and grease an Air fryer basket.
2. Mix the mustard, lemon juice, oil, tarragon, salt, and black pepper in a large bowl.
3. Coat the chops generously with the mustard mixture and arrange in the Air fryer basket.
4. Roast for about 15 minutes, flipping once in between and dish out to serve hot.

Herbed Lamb Chops

SERVES: 2

PREP TIME: 10 minutes
COOK TIME: 15 minutes

1 tsp. dried rosemary
1 tsp. dried thyme
1 tsp. dried oregano
½ tsp. ground cumin
½ tsp. ground coriander
Salt and black pepper, to taste
4 (115 g) lamb chops
15 ml fresh lemon juice
15 ml olive oil

1. Preheat the Air fryer to 200°C and grease an Air fryer basket.
2. Mix the lemon juice, oil, herbs, and spices in a large bowl.
3. Coat the chops generously with the herb mixture and refrigerate to marinate for about 1 hour.
4. Arrange the chops in the Air fryer basket and roast for about 15 minutes, flipping once in between.
5. Dish out the lamb chops in a platter and serve hot.

Simple Lamb Chops

SERVES: 2

PREP TIME: 10 minutes
COOK TIME: 15 minutes

15 ml olive oil
4 (115 g) lamb chops
Salt and black pepper, to taste

1. Preheat the Air fryer to 200°C and grease an Air fryer basket.
2. Mix the olive oil, salt, and black pepper in a large bowl and add chops.
3. Arrange the chops in the Air fryer basket and roast for about 15 minutes.
4. Dish out the lamb chops and serve hot.

Za'atar Lamb Loin Chops

SERVES: 4

PREP TIME: 10 minutes COOK TIME: 15 minutes	5 ml olive oil 1 tbsp. Za'atar Salt and black pepper, to taste 8 (100 g) bone-in lamb loin chops, trimmed 3 garlic cloves, crushed 15 ml fresh lemon juice

1. Preheat the Air fryer to 200°C and grease an Air fryer basket.
2. Mix the garlic, lemon juice, oil, Za'atar, salt, and black pepper in a large bowl.
3. Coat the chops generously with the herb mixture and arrange the chops in the Air fryer basket.
4. Roast for about 15 minutes, flipping twice in between and dish out the lamb chops to serve hot.

(Note: Za'atar - Za'atar is generally made with ground dried thyme, oregano, marjoram, or some combination thereof, mixed with toasted sesame seeds, and salt, though other spices such as sumac might also be added. Some commercial varieties also include roasted flour.)

Pesto Coated Lamb Rack

SERVES: 4

PREP TIME: 15 minutes COOK TIME: 15 minutes	½ bunch fresh mint 60 ml extra-virgin olive oil 10 g honey Salt and black pepper, to taste 1 (680 g) rack of lamb 1 garlic clove

1. Preheat the Air fryer to 200°C and grease an Air fryer basket.
2. Put the mint, garlic, oil, honey, salt, and black pepper in a blender and pulse until smooth to make pesto.
3. Coat the rack of lamb with this pesto on both sides and arrange in the Air fryer basket.
4. Roast for about 15 minutes and cut the rack into individual chops to serve.

Spiced Lamb Steaks

SERVES: 3

PREP TIME: 15 minutes COOK TIME: 15 minutes	½ onion, roughly chopped ½ tsp. ground cumin ½ tsp. ground cinnamon ½ tsp. cayenne pepper Salt and black pepper, to taste 680 g boneless lamb strip steaks 5 garlic cloves, peeled 1 tbsp. fresh ginger, peeled 1 tsp. garam masala 1 tsp. ground fennel

1. Preheat the Air fryer to 165°C and grease an Air fryer basket.
2. Put the onion, garlic, ginger, and spices in a blender and pulse until smooth.
3. Coat the lamb steaks with this mixture on both sides and refrigerate to marinate for about 24 hours.
4. Arrange the lamb steaks in the Air fryer basket and roast for about 15 minutes, flipping once in between.
5. Dish out the steaks in a platter and serve warm.

Lollipop Lamb Chops

SERVES: 4

PREP TIME: 15 minutes
COOK TIME: 7 minutes

½ small clove garlic
15 g packed fresh parsley
50 g packed fresh mint
½ tsp. lemon juice
8 lamb chops (1 rack)
2 tbsps. vegetable oil
Salt and freshly ground black pepper, to taste

1 tbsp. dried rosemary, chopped
1 tbsp. dried thyme
22 g grated Parmesan cheese
50 g shelled pistachios
¼ tsp. salt
120 ml olive oil

1. Make the pesto by combining the garlic, parsley and mint in a food processor and process until finely chopped. Add the lemon juice, Parmesan cheese, pistachios and salt. Process until all the ingredients have turned into a paste. With the processor running, slowly pour the olive oil in. Scrape the sides of the processor with a spatula and process for another 30 seconds.
2. Preheat the air fryer to 200°C. Rub both sides of the lamb chops with vegetable oil and season with salt, pepper, rosemary and thyme, pressing the herbs into the meat gently with the fingers. Transfer the lamb chops to the air fryer basket.
3. Air fry the lamb chops for 5 minutes. Flip the chops over and air fry for an additional 2 minutes.
4. Serve the lamb chops with mint pesto drizzled on top.

Savoury Lamb Meatballs

SERVES: 4

PREP TIME: 20 minutes
COOK TIME: 8 minutes

Meatballs:
2 tsps. fresh oregano, finely chopped
2 tbsps. milk
1 egg yolk
½ small onion, finely diced
1 clove garlic, minced
Salt and freshly ground black pepper, to taste
80 g crumbled feta cheese, for garnish
454 g lamb mince
2 tbsps. fresh parsley, finely chopped (plus more for garnish)
For the Tomato Sauce:
2 tbsps. butter
1 clove garlic, smashed
Salt, to taste
Olive oil, for greasing
Pinch crushed red pepper flakes
¼ tsp. ground cinnamon
1 (794-g) tin crushed tomatoes

1. Combine all ingredients for the meatballs in a large bowl and mix just until everything is combined. Shape the mixture into 3-cm balls or shape the meat between two spoons to make quenelles.
2. Preheat the air fryer to 200°C.
3. While the air fryer is preheating, start the quick tomato sauce. Put the butter, garlic and red pepper flakes in a sauté pan and heat over medium heat on the stovetop. Let the garlic sizzle a little, but before the butter browns, add the cinnamon and tomatoes. Bring to a simmer and simmer for 15 minutes. Season with salt.
4. Grease the bottom of the air fryer basket with olive oil and transfer the meatballs to the air fryer basket in one layer, air frying in batches if necessary.
5. Air fry for 8 minutes, giving the basket a shake once during the cooking process to turn the meatballs over.
6. To serve, spoon a pool of the tomato sauce onto plates and add the meatballs. Sprinkle the feta cheese on top and garnish with more fresh parsley. Serve immediately.

Herbed Lamb Chops and Parmesan

SERVES: 2

PREP TIME: 10 minutes
COOK TIME: 5 minutes

1 large egg
1 tbsp. chopped fresh rosemary leaves
1 tsp. chopped fresh thyme leaves
2 cloves garlic, minced
25 g powdered Parmesan cheese
1 tbsp. chopped fresh oregano leaves
½ tsp. ground black pepper

4 (2-cm-thick) lamb chops
For Garnish/Serving (Optional):
Lavender flowers
Lemon slices
Sprigs of fresh oregano
Sprigs of fresh rosemary
Sprigs of fresh thyme

1. Spray the air fryer basket with avocado oil. Preheat the air fryer to 205°C..
2. Beat the egg in a shallow bowl, add the garlic, and stir well to combine. In another shallow bowl, mix together Parmesan, herbs, and pepper.
3. One at a time, dip the lamb chops into the egg mixture, shake off the excess egg, and then dredge them in the Parmesan mixture. Use your hands to coat the chops well in the Parmesan mixture and form a nice crust on all sides, if necessary, dip the chops again in both the egg and the Parmesan mixture.
4. Place the lamb chops in the air fryer basket, leaving space between them, and roast for 5 minutes, or until the internal temperature reaches 60°C for medium doneness. Allow them to rest for 10 minutes before serving.
5. Garnish with sprigs of oregano, rosemary, and thyme, and lavender flowers, if desired. Serve with lemon slices, if desired.
6. Best served fresh. Store leftovers in an airtight container in the fridge for up to 4 days. Serve chilled over a salad, or reheat in a 175°C air fryer for 3 minutes, or until heated through.

Easy Lamb Burger

SERVES: 3 TO 4

PREP TIME: 15 minutes
COOK TIME: 16 minutes

2 tsps. olive oil
⅓ onion, finely chopped
½ tsp. salt
freshly ground black pepper
4 thick pita breads
toppings and condiments
1 clove garlic, minced
454 g lamb mince
90 g black olives, finely chopped
60 g crumbled feta cheese
2 tbsps. fresh parsley, finely chopped
1½ tsps. fresh oregano, finely chopped

1. Preheat a medium frying pan over medium-high heat on the stovetop. Add the olive oil and cook the onion until tender, but not browned about 4 to 5 minutes. Add the garlic and cook for another minute. Transfer the onion and garlic to a mixing bowl and add the minced lamb, parsley, oregano, olives, feta cheese, salt and pepper. Gently mix the ingredients together.
2. Divide the mixture into 3 or 4 equal portions and then form the hamburgers, being careful not to over-handle the meat. One good way to do this is to throw the meat back and forth between the hands like a baseball, packing the meat each time you catch it. Flatten the balls into patties, making an indentation in the centre of each patty. Flatten the sides of the patties as well to make it easier to fit them into the air fryer basket.
3. Preheat the air fryer to 190°C.
4. If you don't have room for all four burgers, air fry two or three burgers at a time for 8 minutes. Flip the burgers over and air fry for another 8 minutes. If you cooked the burgers in batches, return the first batch of burgers to the air fryer for the last two minutes of cooking to re-heat. This should give you a medium-well burger. If you'd prefer a medium-rare burger, shorten the cooking time to about 13 minutes. Remove the burgers to a resting plate and let the burgers rest for a few minutes before dressing and serving.
5. While the burgers are resting, bake the pita breads in the air fryer for 2 minutes. Tuck the burgers into the toasted pita breads, or wrap the pitas around the burgers and serve with a tzatziki sauce or some mayonnaise.

CHAPTER 7
SNACK

Bacon-Wrapped Prawns / 50

Crunchy Kale Chips / 50

Savoury Spiced Almond / 51

Godlen Avocado Fries / 51

Beery Thai Prawns / 52

Convenient Tortilla Chips / 52

Brussels Sprouts Crisps / 53

Chicken Wings with Berbere Spice / 53

Cauliflower with Bacon Skewers / 54

Parmesan Peppers / 54

Pecorino Toscano and Broccoli Fat Bombs / 54

Bacon with Avocado Egg Bites / 55

Healthy Fried Leek / 55

Crackling Bites / 55

Blooming Onion / 56

Bacon-Wrapped Prawns

SERVES: 10

PREP TIME: 45 minutes
COOK TIME: 8 minutes

1 tbsp. shallot powder
¼ tsp. cumin powder
600g thin bacon slices
600g prawns, peeled and deveined
1 tsp. paprika
1 tbsp. salt
1 tsp. chilli powder
½ tsp. ground black pepper
½ tsp. red pepper flakes, crushed

1. Toss the prawns with all the seasoning until they are coated well.
2. Next, wrap a slice of bacon around the prawns, securing with a toothpick, repeat with the remaining ingredients, chill for 30 minutes.
3. Air-fry them at 180ºC for 7 to 8 minutes, working in batches. Serve with cocktail sticks if desired. Enjoy!

Crunchy Kale Chips

SERVES: 8 CUPS

PREP TIME: 5 minutes
COOK TIME: 10 minutes

½ tsp. dried chives
½ tsp. dried dill
⅛ tsp. fine sea salt
⅛ tsp. ground black pepper
2 large bunches kale
½ tsp. dried parsley
¼ tsp. garlic powder
¼ tsp. onion powder

1. Spray the air fryer basket with avocado oil. Preheat the air fryer to 180ºC.
2. Place the seasonings, salt, and pepper in a small bowl and mix well.
3. Wash the kale and pat completely dry. Use a sharp knife to carve out the thick inner stems, then spray the leaves with avocado oil and sprinkle them with the seasoning mix.
4. Place the kale leaves in the air fryer in a single layer and air fry for 10 minutes, shaking and rotating the chips halfway through. Transfer the baked chips to a baking sheet to cool completely and crisp up. Repeat with the remaining kale. Sprinkle the cooled chips with salt before serving, if desired.
5. Kale chips can be stored in an airtight container at room temperature for up to 1 week, but they are best eaten within 3 days.

Savoury Spiced Almond

SERVES: 4

PREP TIME: 5 minutes
COOK TIME: 6 minutes

160 g raw almonds
50 g raw cashews
¼ tsp. smoked paprika
¼ tsp. onion powder
2 tsps. coconut oil
1 tsp. chilli powder
¼ tsp. cumin

1. In a large bowl, toss all ingredients until nuts are evenly coated with oil and spices. Place nuts into the air fryer basket.
2. Adjust the temperature to 160°C and set the timer for 6 minutes.
3. Toss the fryer basket halfway through the cooking time. Allow to cool completely.

Godlen Avocado Fries

SERVES: 6

PREP TIME: 10 minutes
COOK TIME: 15 minutes

3 firm, barely ripe avocados, halved, peeled, and pitted
200 g Parmesan cheese
1 tsp. paprika
½ tsp. garlic powder
½ tsp. onion powder
2 large eggs
2 tsps. fine sea salt
2 tsps. ground black pepper
2 tsps. ground cumin
1 tsp. chilli powder
140 g panko bread crumbs
Salsa, for serving (optional)
Fresh chopped coriander leaves, for garnish (optional)

1. Spray the air fryer basket with avocado oil. Preheat the air fryer to 205°C.
2. Slice the avocados into thick-cut french fry shapes.
3. In a bowl, mix together the parmesan, salt, bread crumbs, pepper, and seasonings.
4. In a separate shallow bowl, beat the eggs.
5. Dip the avocado fries into the beaten eggs and shake off any excess, then dip them into the parmesan mixture. Use your hands to press the breading into each fry.
6. Spray the fries with avocado oil and place them in the air fryer basket in a single layer, leaving space between them. If there are too many fries to fit in a single layer, work in batches. Air fry for 13 to 15 minutes, until golden brown, flipping after 5 minutes.
7. Serve with salsa, if desired, and garnish with fresh chopped coriander, if desired. Best served fresh.
8. Store leftovers in an airtight container in the fridge for up to 5 days. Reheat in a preheated 205°C air fryer for 3 minutes, or until heated through.

Beery Thai Prawns

SERVES: 4

PREP TIME: 15 minutes
COOK TIME: 8 minutes

16 prawns, cleaned and deveined
1 tsp. baking powder
1 tbsp. curry powder
½ tsp. grated fresh ginger
60 g coconut flour
Salt and ground black pepper, to your liking
½ tsp. cumin powder
1 tsp. fresh lemon juice
1 medium-sized egg, whisked
80 ml beer

1. Toss the prawns with salt, pepper, cumin powder, and lemon juice.
2. In a mixing dish, place the whisked egg, beer, baking powder, curry, and the ginger, mix to combine well.
3. In another mixing dish, place the coconut flour.
4. Now, dip the prawns in the beer mixture, roll your prawns over the coconut flour.
5. Air-fry at 180ºC for 5 minutes, turn them over, press the power button again and bake for additional 2 to 3 minutes. Serve warm!

Convenient Tortilla Chips

SERVES: 2

PREP TIME: 5 minutes
COOK TIME: 3 minutes

Salt, to taste
8 flour tortillas
1 tbsp. olive oil

1. Preheat the air fryer to 200ºC.
2. Slice the flour tortillas into triangles. Coat with a light brushing of olive oil.
3. Put the tortilla pieces in the air fryer basket and air fry for 3 minutes. You may need to do this in batches.
4. Season with salt before serving.

Brussels Sprouts Crisps

SERVES: 4

PREP TIME: 10 minutes
COOK TIME: 15 minutes

1 tsp. fennel seeds
Chopped fresh parsley, for garnish
455 g Brussels sprouts, ends and yellow leaves removed and halved lengthwise
Salt and black pepper, to taste
1 tbsp. toasted sesame oil

1. Place the Brussels sprouts, salt, pepper, sesame oil, and fennel seeds in a resealable plastic bag. Seal the bag and shake to coat.
2. Air-fry at 190ºC for 15 minutes or until tender. Make sure to flip them over halfway through the cooking time.
3. Serve sprinkled with fresh parsley.

Chicken Wings with Berbere Spice

SERVES: 1 DOZEN WINGS

PREP TIME: 5 minutes
COOK TIME: 32 minutes

2 tsps. berbere spice
1 tsp. fine sea salt
1 dozen chicken wings
1 tbsp. coconut oil or bacon fat, melted
For Serving (Omit For Egg-Free):
½ tsp. fine sea salt
¼ tsp. berbere spice
¼ tsp. dried chives
2 hard-boiled eggs

1. Spray the air fryer basket with avocado oil. Preheat the air fryer to 195ºC.
2. Place the chicken wings in a large bowl. Pour the oil over them and turn to coat completely. Sprinkle the berbere and salt on all sides of the chicken.
3. Place the chicken wings in the air fryer and roast for 25 minutes, flipping after 15 minutes.
4. After 25 minutes, increase the temperature to 205ºC and air fry for 6 to 7 minutes or more, until the skin is browned and crisp.
5. While the chicken cooks, prepare the hard-boiled eggs (if using): Peel the eggs, slice them in half, and season them with the salt, berbere, and dried chives. Serve the chicken and eggs together.
6. Store leftovers in an airtight container in the fridge for up to 4 days. Reheat the chicken in a preheated 205ºC air fryer for 5 minutes, or until heated through.

Cauliflower with Bacon Skewers

SERVES: 4

PREP TIME: 10 minutes
COOK TIME: 12 minutes

1½ tbsps. olive oil
¼ tsp. salt
¼ tsp. garlic powder
4 rashers of bacon, cut into thirds
¼ medium brown onion, peeled and cut into 2-cm pieces
115 g (about 8) cauliflower florets

1. Place 1 piece bacon and 2 pieces onion on a 12-cm skewer. Add a second piece bacon, and 2 cauliflower florets, followed by another piece of bacon onto skewer. Repeat with the remaining ingredients and three additional skewers to make four total skewers.
2. Drizzle skewers with olive oil, then sprinkle with salt and garlic powder. Place skewers into ungreased air fryer basket. Adjust the temperature to 190°C and set the timer for 12 minutes, turning the skewers halfway through cooking. When done, vegetables will be tender and bacon will be crispy. Serve warm.

Parmesan Peppers

SERVES: 4

PREP TIME: 20 minutes
COOK TIME: 7 minutes

1 egg, beaten
340g peppers, seeded and cut to ½-cm strips
2 tbsps. olive oil
50 g Parmesan cheese, grated
4 small tomato
1 tsp. sea salt
½ tsp. red pepper flakes, crushed

1. In a mixing bowl, combine together the egg, Parmesan, salt, and red pepper flakes, mix to combine well.
2. Dip peppers into the batter and transfer them to the cooking basket. Brush with the olive oil.
3. Bake in the preheated Air Fryer at 200°C for 4 minutes. Shake the basket and bake for a further 3 minutes. Work in batches.
4. Taste, adjust the seasonings and serve. Serve with tomatoes!

Pecorino Toscano and Broccoli Fat Bombs

SERVES: 6

PREP TIME: 15 minutes
COOK TIME: 15 minutes

110 g bacon bits
100 g Pecorino Toscano, freshly grated
Paprika, to taste
1 large-sized head of broccoli, broken into small florets
½ tsp. sea salt
¼ tsp. ground black pepper, or more to taste
1 tbsp. Shoyu sauce
1 tsp. groundnut oil

1. Add the broccoli florets to boiling water, boil for approximately 4 minutes, drain well.
2. Season with salt and pepper, drizzle with Shoyu sauce and groundnut oil. Mash with a potato masher.
3. Add the bacon and cheese to the mixture, shape the mixture into bite-sized balls.
4. Air-fry at 200°C for 10 minutes, shake the Air Fryer basket, push the power button again, and continue to bake for 5 minutes or more.
5. Toss the fried keto bombs with paprika. Serve warm!

Bacon with Avocado Egg Bites

SERVES: 4

PREP TIME: 20 minutes
COOK TIME: 13 minutes

2 tbsps. unsalted butter, softened
2 tbsps. mayonnaise
1 red chilli, seeded and finely chopped
2 tbsps. chopped fresh coriander
Juice of ½ lime
Salt and freshly ground black pepper
170 g middle bacon
2 hard-boiled eggs, chopped
Flesh of ½ avocado, chopped

1. Arrange the bacon in a single layer in the air fryer basket (it's OK if the bacon sits a bit on the sides). Set the air fryer to 175°C and air fry for 10 minutes. Check for crispiness and air fry for 2 to 3 minutes longer if needed. Transfer the bacon to a paper towel–lined plate and let it cool completely. Reserve 2 tbsps. of bacon grease from the bottom of the air fryer basket. Finely chop the bacon and set aside in a small, shallow bowl.
2. In a large bowl, combine the eggs, avocado, butter, mayonnaise, red chilli, coriander, and lime juice. Mash into a smooth paste with a fork or potato smasher. Season to taste with salt and pepper.
3. Add the reserved bacon grease to the egg mixture and stir gently until thoroughly combined. Cover and refrigerate for 30 minutes, or until the mixture is firm.
4. Divide the mixture into 12 equal portions and shape into balls. Roll the balls in the chopped bacon bits until completely coated.

Healthy Fried Leek

SERVES: 4

PREP TIME: 15 minutes
COOK TIME: 10 minutes

50 g almond flour
½ tsp. baking powder
50 g Parmesan cheese
1 large-sized leek, cut into 1-cm wide rings
Salt and pepper, to taste
1 tsp. mustard
240 ml milk
1 egg

1. Toss your leeks with salt and pepper.
2. In a mixing bowl, whisk the mustard, milk and egg until frothy and pale.
3. Now, combine almond flour and baking powder in another mixing bowl. In the third bowl, place the parmesan
4. Coat the leek slices with the almond flour mixture. Dredge the floured leek slices into the milk/egg mixture, coating well. Finally, roll them over the parmesan.
5. Air-fry for approximately 10 minutes at 190ºC. Serve warm!

Crackling Bites

SERVES: 10

PREP TIME: 5 minutes
COOK TIME: 16 minutes

1 tbsp. sea salt
2 tbsps. smoked paprika
455 g pork rind raw, scored by the butcher

1. Sprinkle and rub salt on the skin side of the pork rind. Allow it to sit for 30 minutes.
2. Roast at 190ºC for 8 minutes, turn them over and roast for a further 8 minutes or until blistered.
3. Sprinkle the smoked paprika all over the pork crackling and serve.

Blooming Onion

SERVES: 8

PREP TIME: 10 minutes
COOK TIME: 35 minutes

1 extra-large onion (about 6-cm in diameter)
2 large eggs
1 tsp. garlic powder
¼ tsp. cayenne pepper
¼ tsp. fine sea salt
1 tbsp. water
50 g powdered Parmesan cheese
2 tsps. paprika
¼ tsp. ground black pepper
For Garnish (Optional):
Fresh parsley leaves
Powdered Parmesan cheese
For Serving (Optional):
Ranch Dressing
Reduced-sugar or sugar-free ketchup
Prepared yellow mustard

1. Spray the air fryer basket with avocado oil. Preheat the air fryer to 175°C.
2. Using a sharp knife, cut the top 1-cm off the onion and peel off the outer layer. Cut the onion into 8 equal sections, stopping 2-cm from the bottom—you want the onion to stay together at the base. Gently spread the sections, or "petals," apart.
3. Crack the eggs into a large bowl, add the water, and whisk well. Place the onion in the dish and coat it well in the egg. Use a spoon to coat the inside of the onion and all of the petals.
4. In a small bowl, combine the Parmesan, seasonings, salt, and pepper.
5. Place the onion in a 12-cm pie dish or casserole dish. Sprinkle the seasoning mixture all over the onion and use your fingers to press it into the petals. Spray the onion with avocado oil.
6. Loosely cover the onion with parchment paper and then foil. Place the dish in the air fryer. Bake for 30 minutes, then remove it from the air fryer and increase the air fryer temperature to 205°C..
7. Remove the foil and parchment and spray the onion with avocado oil again. Protecting your hands with oven-safe gloves or a tea towel, transfer the onion to the air fryer basket. Bake for an additional 3 to 5 minutes, until light brown and crispy.
8. Garnish with fresh parsley and powdered Parmesan, if desired. Serve with mustard, ranch dressing, and ketchup, if desired.
9. Store leftovers in an airtight container in the fridge for up to 4 days. Reheat in a preheated 205°C. air fryer for 3 to 5 minutes, until warm and crispy.

CHAPTER 8
DESSERT

Swiss Strawberry Roll / 58

Baked Chocolate Cheesecake / 58

Crusted Mini Cheesecake / 59

Perfect Apple Pie / 59

Raspberry with Chocolate Cake / 60

Coconut with Chocolate Cake / 60

Cranberry Butter Cake / 61

Chocolate Muffins / 61

Pecan with Mixed Berries Streusel / 62

Berry Compote and Coconut Chips / 62

Fiesta Pastries / 62

Mozzarella Pretzels / 63

Macadamia Bar / 63

Delicious Mint Pie / 63

Swiss Strawberry Roll

SERVES: 6

PREP TIME: 20 minutes
COOK TIME: 12 minutes

120 g milk
1 egg, at room temperature
¼ tsp. salt
100 g almond flour
5 g sweetener
1 tbsp. yeast
55 g butter, at room temperature
115 g coconut flour
240 g fresh strawberry

Filling:
¼ tsp. ground cinnamon
1 tsp. vanilla paste
10 g sweetener
2 tbsps. butter
4 tbsps. sweetener
1 tsp. ground star anise

1. Heat the milk in a microwave safe bowl and transfer the warm milk to the bowl of a stand electric mixer. Add the sweetener and yeast, and mix to combine well. Cover and let it sit until the yeast is foamy.
2. Then, beat the butter on low speed. Fold in the egg and mix again. Add salt and flour. Mix on medium speed until a soft dough forms.
3. Knead the dough on a lightly floured surface. Cover it loosely and let it sit in a warm place for about 1 hour or until doubled in size. Then, spritz the bottom and sides of a baking pan with cooking oil (butter flavoured).
4. Roll your dough out into a rectangle.
5. Spread 2 tbsps. of butter all over the dough. In a mixing dish, combine 4 tbsps. of sweetener, ground star anise, cinnamon, strawberries, and vanilla, sprinkle evenly over the dough.
6. Then, roll up your dough to form a log. Cut into 6 equal rolls and place them in the parchment-lined Air Fryer basket.
7. Bake at 175ºC or 12 minutes, turning them halfway through the cooking time. Dust with confectioners' sweetener and enjoy!

Baked Chocolate Cheesecake

SERVES: 6

PREP TIME: 40 minutes
COOK TIME: 35 minutes

5 g powdered sweetener
½ tsp. vanilla paste
1 egg, at room temperature
60 g almond flour
1½ tbsps. unsalted butter, melted
2 tbsps. sweetener
1 (230-g) package cream cheese, softened
50 g chocolate powder
Topping:
345 g sour cream
3 tbsps. powdered sweetener
1 tsp. vanilla extract

1. Thoroughly combine the almond flour, butter, chocolate powder, and 2 tbsps. of sweetener in a mixing bowl. Press the mixture into the bottom of lightly greased custard cups.
2. Then, mix the cream cheese, ¼ powdered sweetener, vanilla, and egg using an electric mixer on low speed. Pour the batter into the pan, covering the crust.
3. Bake in the preheated Air Fryer at 165ºC for 35 minutes until edges are puffed and the surface is firm.
4. Mix the sour cream, 3 tbsps. of powdered sweetener, and vanilla for the topping, spread over the crust and allow it to cool to room temperature.
5. Transfer to your refrigerator for 6 to 8 hours. Serve well chilled.

CHAPTER 8: DESSERT

Crusted Mini Cheesecake

SERVES: 8

PREP TIME: 30 minutes
COOK TIME: 18 minutes

For the Crust:
150 g almond flour
8 tbsps. melted butter
⅓ tsp. grated nutmeg
1½ tbsps. sweetener
1 tsp. ground cinnamon

A pinch of salt, to taste
For the Cheesecake:
2 eggs
10 g Sweetener
½ tsp. vanilla essence
85 g unsweetened chocolate chips
1½ tbsps. sour cream
115 g soft cheese

1. Firstly, line eight cups of mini muffin pan with paper liners.
2. To make the crust, mix the almond flour together with sweetener, cinnamon, nutmeg, and salt.
3. Now, add melted butter and stir well to moisten the crumb mixture.
4. Divide the crust mixture among the muffin cups and press gently to make even layers.
5. In another bowl, whip together the soft cheese, sour cream and Sweetener until uniform and smooth. Fold in the eggs and the vanilla essence.
6. Then, divide chocolate chips among the prepared muffin cups. Then, add the cheese mix to each muffin cup.
7. Bake for about 18 minutes at 175ºC. Bake in batches if needed. To finish, transfer the mini cheesecakes to a cooling rack, store in the fridge.

Perfect Apple Pie

SERVES: 6

PREP TIME: 15 minutes
COOK TIME: 30 minutes

1 frozen shortcrust pastry, thawed
1 large apple, peeled, cored and chopped
45 g icing sugar, divided
1 tbsp. ground cinnamon
2 tsps. fresh lemon juice
½ tsp. vanilla extract
15 g butter, chopped
1 egg, beaten

1. Preheat the Air fryer to 160ºC and grease a pie dish lightly.
2. Cut 2 crusts, first about ½-cm larger than pie dish and second, a little smaller than first one. Arrange the large crust in the bottom of pie dish.
3. Mix apple, 30 g of sugar, cinnamon, lemon juice and vanilla extract in a large bowl.
4. Put the apple mixture evenly over the bottom crust and top with butter.
5. Arrange the second crust on top and seal the edges.
6. Cut 4 slits in the top crust carefully and brush with egg.
7. Sprinkle with sugar and arrange the pie dish in the Air fryer basket.
8. Bake for about 30 minutes and dish out to serve.

Raspberry with Chocolate Cake

SERVES: 4

PREP TIME: 15 minutes
COOK TIME: 27 minutes

10 g sweetener
55 g unsalted butter, room temperature
½ tsp. ground cinnamon
1 tbsp. candied ginger
⅛ tsp. table salt
1 egg plus 1 egg white, lightly whisked

85 g almond flour
2 tbsps. cocoa powder
For the Filling:
60 g fresh raspberries
10 g sweetener
1 tsp. fresh lime juice

1. Firstly, set your Air Fryer to cook at 160°C. Then, spritz the inside of two cake pans with the butter-flavoured cooking spray.
2. In a mixing bowl, beat the sweetener and butter until creamy and uniform. Then, stir in the whisked eggs. Stir in the almond flour, cocoa powder, cinnamon, ginger and salt.
3. Press the batter into the cake pans, use a wide spatula to level the surface of the batter. Bake for 20 minutes or until a wooden stick inserted in the centre of the cake comes out completely dry.
4. While your cake is baking, stir together all of the ingredients for the filling in a medium saucepan. Cook over high heat, stirring frequently and mashing with the back of a spoon, bring to a boil and decrease the temperature.
5. Continue to cook, stirring until the mixture thickens, for another 7 minutes. Let the filling cool to room temperature.
6. Spread ½ of raspberry filling over the first crust. Top with another crust, spread remaining filling over top. Spread frosting over top and sides of your cake. Enjoy!

Coconut with Chocolate Cake

SERVES: 6

PREP TIME: 10 minutes
COOK TIME: 15 minutes

A pinch of fine sea salt
2 eggs, whisked
½ tsp. vanilla extract
55 g butter, at room temperature
85 g chocolate, unsweetened and chopped
1 tbsp. liquid stevia
180 g coconut flour

1. Begin by preheating your Air Fryer to 165°C.
2. In a microwave-safe bowl, melt the butter, chocolate, and stevia.
3. Add the other ingredients to the cooled chocolate mixture, stir to combine well. Scrape the batter into a lightly greased baking pan.
4. Bake in the preheated Air Fryer for 15 minutes or until the centre is springy and a toothpick comes out dry. Enjoy!

Cranberry Butter Cake

SERVES: 8

PREP TIME: 30 minutes
COOK TIME: 20 minutes

100 g almond flour
115 g butter
½ tsp. vanilla paste
2 eggs plus 1 egg yolk, beaten
⅓ tsp. baking soda
⅓ tsp. baking powder
15 g sweetener
½ tsp. ground cloves
⅓ tsp. ground cinnamon
½ tsp. cardamom
50 g cranberries, fresh or thawed
1 tbsp. browned butter
For Ricotta Frosting:
¼ tsp. salt
Zest of ½ lemon
115 g butter
125 g firm Ricotta cheese
20 g powdered sweetener

1. Start by preheating your Air Fryer to 180ºC.
2. In a mixing bowl, combine the flour with baking soda, baking powder, sweetener, ground cloves, cinnamon, and cardamom.
3. In a separate bowl, whisk butter with vanilla paste, mix in the eggs until light and fluffy. Add the flour and sugar mixture to the butter, then add egg mixture. Fold in the cranberries and browned butter.
4. Scrape the mixture into the greased cake pan. Then, bake in the preheated Air Fryer for about 20 minutes.
5. Meanwhile, in a food processor, whip 55 g of the butter and Ricotta cheese until there are no lumps.
6. Slowly add the powdered sweetener and salt until your mixture has reached a thick consistency. Stir in the lemon zest, mix to combine and chill completely before using.
7. Frost the cake and enjoy!

Chocolate Muffins

SERVES: 8

PREP TIME: 10 minutes
COOK TIME: 10 minutes

200 g plain flour
2 tsps. baking powder
1 egg
245 g yoghurt
80 g mini chocolate chips
50 g icing sugar
Salt, to taste
80 ml rapeseed oil
2 tsps. vanilla extract

1. Preheat the Air fryer to 180ºC and grease 8 muffin cups lightly.
2. Mix flour, baking powder, sugar and salt in a bowl.
3. Whisk egg, oil, yoghurt and vanilla extract in another bowl.
4. Combine the flour and egg mixtures and mix until a smooth mixture is formed. Fold in the chocolate chips and divide this mixture into the prepared muffin cups.
5. Transfer into the Air fryer basket and bake for about 10 minutes.
6. Refrigerate for 2 hours and serve chilled.

Pecan with Mixed Berries Streusel

SERVES: 3

PREP TIME: 15 minutes
COOK TIME: 17 minutes

1 egg
2 tbsps. cold salted butter, cut into pieces
80 g mixed berries
3 tbsps. pecans, chopped
3 tbsps. almonds, slivered
2 tbsps. walnuts, chopped
3 tbsps. granulated sweetener
½ tsp. ground cinnamon

1. Mix your nuts, sweetener, cinnamon, egg, and butter until well combined.
2. Place mixed berries on the bottom of a lightly greased Air Fryer-safe dish. Top with the prepared topping.
3. Bake at 170°C for 17 minutes. Serve at room temperature.

Berry Compote and Coconut Chips

SERVES: 6

PREP TIME: 15 minutes
COOK TIME: 20 minutes

1 tbsp. butter
½ tsp. ground cinnamon
1 tsp. pure vanilla extract
45 g coconut chips
340 g mixed berries
10 g granulated sweetener
¼ tsp. grated nutmeg
¼ tsp. ground cloves

1. Start by preheating your Air Fryer to 165°C. Grease a baking pan with butter.
2. Place all ingredients, except for the coconut chips, in a baking pan. Bake in the preheated Air Fryer for 20 minutes.
3. Serve in individual bowls, garnished with coconut chips.

Fiesta Pastries

SERVES: 8

PREP TIME: 15 minutes
COOK TIME: 20 minutes

200 g prepared frozen puff pastry, cut into 16 squares
½ of apple, peeled, cored and chopped
1 tsp. fresh orange zest, grated finely
½ tbsp. white sugar
½ tsp. ground cinnamon

1. Preheat the Air fryer to 200°C and grease an Air fryer basket.
2. Mix all ingredients in a bowl except puff pastry. Arrange about 1 tsp. of this mixture in the centre of each square.
3. Fold each square into a triangle and slightly press the edges with a fork.
4. Arrange the pastries in the Air fryer basket and bake for about 10 minutes.
5. Dish out and serve immediately.

Mozzarella Pretzels

SERVES: 6

PREP TIME: 10 minutes COOK TIME: 10 minutes	5 g granular sweetener, divided 1 tsp. ground cinnamon 170 g desiccated Mozzarella cheese 100 g blanched finely ground almond flour 2 tbsps. salted butter, melted, divided

1. Place Mozzarella, flour, 1 tbsp. of butter, and 2 tbsps. of sweetener in a large microwave-safe bowl. Microwave on high 45 seconds, then stir with a fork until a smooth dough ball forms.
2. Separate dough into six equal sections. Gently roll each section into a 24-cm rope, then fold into a pretzel shape.
3. Place pretzels into ungreased air fryer basket. Adjust the temperature to 190°C and set the timer for 8 minutes, turning pretzels halfway through cooking.
4. In a small bowl, combine remaining butter, remaining sweetener, and cinnamon. Brush ½ mixture on both sides of pretzels.
5. Place pretzels back into air fryer and bake for an additional 2 minutes at 190°C.
6. Transfer pretzels to a large plate. Brush on both sides with remaining butter mixture, then let it cool 5 minutes before serving.

Macadamia Bar

SERVES: 10

PREP TIME: 15 minutes COOK TIME: 30 minutes	3 tbsps. butter, softened 1 tsp. baking powder 1 tsp. apple cider vinegar 165 g coconut flour 3 tbsps. Sweetener 1 tsp. vanilla extract 2 eggs, beaten 50 g macadamia nuts, chopped Cooking spray

1. Spray the air fryer basket with cooking spray.
2. Then mix all remaining ingredients in the mixing bowl and stir until you get a homogenous mixture.
3. Pour the mixture in the air fryer basket and bake at 175°C for 30 minutes.
4. When the mixture is cooked, cut it into bars and transfer in the serving plates.

Delicious Mint Pie

SERVES: 2

PREP TIME: 15 minutes COOK TIME: 25 minutes	1 tsp. spearmint, dried 4 tsps. coconut flour Cooking spray 1 tbsp. instant coffee 2 tbsps. almond butter, softened 2 tbsps. sweetener 1 tsp. dried mint 3 eggs, beaten

1. Spray the air fryer basket with cooking spray.
2. Then mix all ingredients in the mixer bowl.
3. When you get a smooth mixture, transfer it in the air fryer basket. Flatten it gently.
4. Bake the pie at 185°C for 25 minutes.

APPENDIX: RECIPES INDEX

A
apple
Apple and Walnut Muffins / 6
Apple Bread Rolls / 4
Fiesta Pastries / 62
Perfect Apple Pie / 59
asparagus
Asparagus Bundles Enveloped in Crunchy Bacon Strips / 37
aubergine
Aubergine with Tomato and Cheese / 37
Avocado
Avocado Quesadillas / 4
Bacon with Avocado Egg Bites / 55
Godlen Avocado Fries / 51

B
Banana
Banana Bread / 6
beef
Gourmet Meatloaf / 16
Herbed Beef Roast / 13
Simple Beef Burgers / 14
beef eye of round
Beef Roast / 15
Beef Short Rib
Grilled Beef Short Ribs / 15
beef silverside
Beef Tips and Onion / 17
Crispy Strip Steak / 17
beef steak
Delicious Simple Steaks / 13
Simple New York Strip Steak / 12
Steak with Peppers / 16
Broccoli
Grilled Broccoli Frittata / 7
Brussels sprout
Brussels Sprouts Crisps / 53

C
Carrot
Easy Glazed Carrots / 36
Cauliflower
Cauliflower with Avocado / 5
Cauliflower with Bacon Skewers / 54
chestnut mushroom
Courgette and Mushroom Kebab / 36
Mushrooms with Peas / 39
Chicken Wing
Chicken Wings with Berbere Spice / 53
Coconut
Coconut with Chocolate Cake / 60
Cod
Sweet and Sour Glazed Cod / 22
Zesty Spicy Cod / 20
courgette
Cold Salad with Pasta and Veggies / 40
Courgette and Mushroom Bread / 8
Roast Aubergine with Courgette Bites / 40
Savoury Vegetable Salsa Wraps / 9
Cranberry
Cranberry Butter Cake / 61

F
filet mignon
Buttered Filet Mignon / 12
Streaky Rasher Wrapped Filet Mignon / 17

G
Gammon
Gammon and Corn Muffins / 7

H
Haddock
Baked Haddock / 23
Halibut
Curried Halibut / 21

K
Kale
Crunchy Kale Chips / 50

L
lamb
Easy Lamb Burger / 48
Savoury Lamb Meatballs / 47
Lamb Chop
Herbed Lamb Chops / 45

Herbed Lamb Chops and Parmesan / 48
Lime Marinated Lamb Chop / 42
Lollipop Lamb Chops / 47
Simple Lamb Chops / 45
Lamb leg
Lamb leg with Brussels Sprouts / 43
Roasted Lamb / 43
Lamb Loin Chop
Mustard Lamb Loin Chops / 44
Za'atar Lamb Loin Chops / 46
Lamb Rack
Pesto Coated Lamb Rack / 46
Lamb Rib
Grilled Lamb Ribs / 42
lamb steak
Quick Lamb Satay / 44
Spiced Lamb Steaks / 46

M
Mahi Mahi
Mahi Mahi and Runner beans / 24

P
pork
Pork with Pinto Bean Gorditas / 32
pork chop
Cheese Crusted Chops / 32
Healthy Pork Chop Stir Fry / 30
Savoury Mexican Pork Chops / 27
Vietnamese Pork Chops / 26
pork loin
Roast Citrus Pork Loin / 31
pork rib
Barbecue Pork Ribs / 28
BBQ Pork Ribs / 26
Pork Steak
BBQ Pork Steaks / 28
Pork Tenderloin
Marinated Pork Tenderloin / 29
Orange Pork Tenderloin / 27
Pork Tenderloin with Radicchio and Endive Salad / 33
Simple Pulled Pork / 29

potato
Homemade Favourite Potatoes / 39
Prawn
Bacon-Wrapped Prawns / 50
Beery Thai Prawns / 52
Pumpkin
British Pumpkin Egg Bake / 10
Veggie-filled Pumpkin Basket / 39

R
Raspberry
Raspberry with Chocolate Cake / 60
rib eye steak
Buttered Rib Eye Steak / 14

S
Salmon
Cajun Spiced Salmon / 22
Simple Grilled Salmon / 20
Shrimp
Paprika Shrimp / 21
skirt steak
Traditional Skirt Steak Strips with Veggies / 16
spinach
Cheddar Bacon Burst and Spinach / 30
Spinach Cheese Casserole / 38
Strawberry
Swiss Strawberry Roll / 58

T
tofu
Incredibly Crunchy Tofu / 35
tomato
Fried Fresh Veggie Medley / 40
Tuna
Tuna Patties with Cheese Sauce / 19
Tuna with Red Onions and Herbs / 23

W
White Fish
Cauliflower with White Fish Cakes / 24

BASIC KITCHEN CONVERSIONS & EQUIVALENTS

DRY MEASUREMENTS CONVERSION CHART
3 teaspoons = 1 tablespoon = 1/16 cup
6 teaspoons = 2 tablespoons = 1/8 cup
12 teaspoons = 4 tablespoons = ¼ cup
24 teaspoons = 8 tablespoons = ½ cup
36 teaspoons = 12 tablespoons = ¾ cup
48 teaspoons = 16 tablespoons = 1 cup

METRIC TO US COOKING CONVERSIONS

OVEN TEMPERATURES
120 °C = 250 °F
160 °C = 320 °F
180 °C = 350 °F
205 °C = 400 °F
220 °C = 425 °F

LIQUID MEASUREMENTS CONVERSION CHART
8 fluid ounces = 1 cup = ½ pint = ¼ quart
16 fluid ounces = 2 cups = 1 pint = ½ quart
32 fluid ounces = 4 cups = 2 pints = 1 quart = ¼ gallon
128 fluid ounces = 16 cups = 8 pints = 4 quarts = 1 gallon

BAKING IN GRAMS
1 cup flour = 140 grams
1 cup sugar = 150 grams
1 cup powdered sugar = 160 grams
1 cup heavy cream = 235 grams

VOLUME
1 milliliter = 1/5 teaspoon
5 ml = 1 teaspoon
15 ml = 1 tablespoon
240 ml = 1 cup or 8 fluid ounces
1 liter = 34 fluid ounces

WEIGHT
1 gram = .035 ounces
100 grams = 3.5 ounces
500 grams = 1.1 pounds
1 kilogram = 35 ounces

US TO METRIC COOKING CONVERSIONS

1/5 tsp = 1 ml
1 tsp = 5 ml
1 tbsp = 15 ml
1 fluid ounces = 30 ml
1 cup = 237 ml
1 pint (2 cups) = 473 ml
1 quart (4 cups) = .95 liter
1 gallon (16 cups) = 3.8 liters
1 oz = 28 grams
1 pound = 454 grams

BUTTER
1 cup butter = 2 sticks = 8 ounces = 230 grams = 16 tablespoons

WHAT DOES 1 CUP EQUAL
1 cup = 8 fluid ounces
1 cup = 16 tablespoons
1 cup = 48 teaspoons
1 cup = ½ pint
1 cup = ¼ quart
1 cup = 1/16 gallon
1 cup = 240 ml

BAKING PAN CONVERSIONS
9-inch round cake pan = 12 cups
10-inch tube pan =16 cups
10-inch bundt pan = 12 cups
9-inch springform pan = 10 cups
9 x 5 inch loaf pan = 8 cups
9-inch square pan = 8 cups

BAKING PAN CONVERSIONS
1 cup all-purpose flour = 4.5 oz
1 cup rolled oats = 3 oz
1 large egg = 1.7 oz
1 cup butter = 8 oz
1 cup milk = 8 oz
1 cup heavy cream = 8.4 oz
1 cup granulated sugar = 7.1 oz
1 cup packed brown sugar = 7.75 oz
1 cup vegetable oil = 7.7 oz
1 cup unsifted powdered sugar = 4.4 oz

Printed in Great Britain
by Amazon